Methods and Practice of
Elizabethan Swordplay

Methods and Practice of

Elizabethan Swordplay

Craig Turner and Tony Soper

With a Foreword by Joseph Papp

Southern Illinois University Press

Carbondale

Southern Illinois University Press
www.siupress.com

Cover illustration: Figure 2, page 30. (By permission of the Folger Shakespeare
Library)

Illustrations preceding chapters 2, 3, and 4 are reproduced from Giacomo Di
Grassi's *True Arte*, Vincentio Saviolo's *Practise in Two Bookes*, and George
Silver's *Paradoxes of Defence*, by permission of the Folger Shakespeare
Library.

Library of Congress Cataloging-in-Publication Data
Names: Turner, Craig, M.F.A., author. | Soper, Tony, 1939– author.
Title: Methods and practice of Elizabethan swordplay / Craig Turner and
Tony Soper ; with a foreword by Joseph Papp.
Description: Paperback edition. | Carbondale, IL : Southern Illinois University
Press, [2016] | Includes bibliographical references and index.
Identifiers: LCCN 2015047865 | ISBN 9780809335183 (pbk. : alk. paper) |
ISBN 9780809382156 (e-book)
Subjects: LCSH: Fencing—England—History—16th century. | Swordplay—
England—History—16th century. | Dueling—England—History—16th
century. | Great Britain—History—Elizabeth, 1558–1603.
Classification: LCC U860 .T87 2016 | DDC 796.860942/09031—dc23 LC
record available at http://lccn.loc.gov/2015047865

Printed on recycled paper. ♻

Contents

Figures

Foreword

Joseph Papp

DURING MY career as producer and director of the New York Shakespeare Festival, I have constantly tried to relate the essence of Shakespeare to modern audiences. The theatre is active and dynamic. I look for scholarship that makes a difference in the theatre.

Methods and Practice of Elizabethan Swordplay is a fine example of solid scholarship that makes a difference in performance. Stage fights in Shakespeare are always problematic. We want to make them "real" to a modern audience. But we have also suspected that fighting in Shakespeare's day must have had a particular look and feel. Up to now we have had little direct knowledge of how fighting was taught or how the old fencing masters passed on their knowledge.

Craig Turner and Tony Soper have painstakingly analyzed the old English manuals, organizing the ideas and techniques into a readable format, free of the early modern English variants in spelling and grammar. But they have not stopped there. They have also tried to show how early swordplay worked in the context of Shakespeare's culture. They illuminate an aspect of everyday life in Elizabethan England unfamiliar to many of us.

In addition, the authors explain numerous references to sword techniques in plays of the period. Actors and directors can use these explanations to re-charge their visions of the plays. This kind of research brings new insight to many scenes of violence in the plays of the period. *Methods and Practice of Elizabethan Swordplay* is a scholarly work that also serves as a suggestive guide to theatrical staging.

Acknowledgments

THE AUTHORS gratefully acknowledge the invaluable assistance of the staff of the Folger Shakespeare Library in Washington, D.C., in tracking down numerous sixteenth-century items. In addition, we would like to thank the photography department at the Folger for providing original photos for inclusion in this book. Thanks also to Mr. Joseph Papp, producer of the New York Shakespeare Festival, for his encouragement and the foreword. Mr. Leonid Tarassuk, senior research associate in arms and armor at the Metropolitan Museum of Art suggested superb technical corrections for the manuscript.

Mr. Soper would like to thank Mr. Paddy Crean, the renowned fight master, for his encouragement and inspiration, and Mr. Malcolm Ransom, British fight director, for his suggestions regarding the problems of historical accuracy in stage fights.

Mr. Turner would like to thank the University of North Carolina–Chapel Hill for providing a Junior Faculty Development Fund Grant that funded the initial research for this book, an Arts and Humanities Faculty Research Fellowship Award for travel and research expenses, and a grant from the UNC Endowment Committee for Scholarly Publications, Artistic Exhibitions, and Performances for their help in defraying editing, photography, and copying costs. In addition, Mr. Turner would like to thank Dr. Milly Barranger, chair of the Department of Dramatic Art at UNC–Chapel Hill for her encouragement and expert scholarly advice, and Mr. David Hammond, artistic director of Playmakers Repertory Company and professor in the Department of Dramatic Art for his unfailing enthusiasm and support.

Finally, we thank Stephanie and Ginny for their forbearance and kind words.

Introduction

SWORD FIGHTING in movies, television, and live drama has a powerful effect on the popular conception of what swordplay might have been in the past. After watching film stars from Errol Flynn and Douglas Fairbanks to Michael York and Oliver Reed in various period pieces, it must appear to the average modern viewer that swordplay has remained astonishingly similar in look and technique for the last four centuries. The fact is, much of what is done in modern film and theatre productions bears little resemblance to swordplay as Elizabethans knew and practiced it. A close look at Hollywood's so-called swashbuckling style reveals that the kinds of weapons used in modern productions are frequently not accurate to the period. In addition, the fight choreography is often a mishmash of modern (1930s) competitive fencing techniques with a dash of acrobatics thrown in for variety.

Modern directors, usually conscientious about accurately re-creating a period, give up all questions of authority to the modern fight choreographer who may be working from a melange of knowledge, half-truths, and invention to create his fights. From the unfortunate choreographer's point of view, he may be asked to re-create accurate fights—for a medieval *Macbeth,* for instance—with modern fencing foils. The scholarly world has added little insight to this problem through text analysis. Critics and scholars of the Renaissance, who would not hesitate to further investigate almost any word, punctuation, or stage direction in Shakespeare , have been surprisingly mute about such open-ended notations as "they fight," demonstrating, in the words of M. I. Finley, that the study of physical activity is "perhaps the most remarkable of all existing academic taboos" (Brailsford 1).

But how people choose to defend themselves is as much a part of national character as literature, costumes, or cooking. In spite of our unease with such violent martial topics, swordplay is as deserving of study. We cannot completely understand the Elizabethans—or people of any period, for that matter—if we do not understand how they regarded the use of violence and why they employed the self-defense techniques they did. As a consequence, in order to understand the historical, social, and theoretical contexts in which Elizabethan swordplay flourished and developed, and in order to re-create true Elizabethan rapier swordplay for the modern theatre and film, "most modern ideas of swordsmanship should be dismissed" and the original fighting texts should be studied (Castle 3).

Alfred Hutton has said, the rapier "was not an invention, it was a development" (*The Sword and the Centuries* 72). Its introduction to England sparked an intensive reevaluation of all the theory and practice of individual fighting that had gone before, eventually supplanting the much-heralded traditional English sword. A weapon of great popularity on the continent, the rapier was more effectively lethal than anything else available to the everyday man. Its widespread acceptance in England by 1600 forced a popular reappraisal of fighting discipline, training, and offensive strategy.

The rapier's introduction and rapid adoption into English culture can be traced in the literature of the period, and many references in Elizabethan plays become clearer when the original historic and technical swordplay contexts are understood. Knowing this, we can more fully understand how numerous Elizabethan authors relied upon a general knowledge of and interest in rapier techniques in their works. Shakespeare, Marlowe, Tourner, Middleton, and others (like good playwrights of every period) were sensitive to the latest trends and styles and used the rapier vs. sword controversy in their works.

Further, and even more importantly, by looking at a fundamental change in the nature of swordplay, we can explore what Arthur Wise calls "the motivating force behind much personal combat—individual aggression, individual violence" (*The Art and History of Personal Combat* 9–10). More than one writer has commented on the particularly high level of personal violence in the late sixteenth century. The increased use of the rapier, new tactics for swordplay, the development of the rules of dueling, and the social/political tenor of the time (as we shall see) account for this observed effect. Precisely how men have decided to express violence is a neglected part of social history, particularly for times as eventful as the Elizabethan age. There have been many studies on such major martial events as the defeat of the Spanish Armada and the development of new mass warfare techniques for the late sixteenth century. This book, in contrast, will explore a relatively little understood part of everyday violence in English culture around 1600: sword and rapier fighting.

Previous attempts to analyze the fighting styles and weaponry of the period have come either from writers concentrating on literary/textual matters (see Soens, Dessen), or from modern specialists interested in technical fighting matters (Aylward, Hutton). In contrast, *Methods and Practice of Elizabethan Swordplay* is an attempt to reconstruct the theory and mechanics of rapier swordplay—the dominant mode of personal combat in late sixteenth-century England—from the texts that actually describe it. By studying fencing texts that still exist from that era—particularly those that had been written in or translated into English by 1600 (George Silver, Giacomo Di Grassi, and Vincentio Saviolo) and that, as a consequence, would have been available to a wider English audience—we can more accurately visualize personal combat in that time. We can then begin to understand not only why the rapier style was such a revolutionary fighting development, but also something of the ambivalent English attitudes to this new weapon.

Tracing the development of fight techniques as well as the changing terminology of fight vocabulary, we can better assess how the English upper classes—mimicking the enthusiastic use of the rapier on the continent—adopted the rapier in settling private quarrels. Once the upper classes had accepted it, rapier swordplay rapidly entered the popular culture.

This book is an attempt (1) to compare and contrast what we know of early Elizabethan combat practice with the revolutionary rapier influences from Europe, just before 1600, (2) to reconstruct rapier fighting technique by comparing the ideas of Di Grassi, Saviolo, and Silver, and (3) to suggest a typical Elizabethan style for swordplay as it might have appeared in the streets, alleys, and early-morning fields. In quoting from the three fencing manuals, we have modernized spellings and, occasionally, added punctuation where we felt it helps clarity. Also, all quotes from Shakespeare are taken from *The Complete Pelican Shakespeare,* general editor Alfred Harbage (Baltimore, 1971).

Although we cursorily trace some aspects of weapon development to earlier times, the period of focus for us is approximately 1550 to 1605, the Elizabethan period. Rapier play had swept the continent years earlier, but this is the story of the rapier as it was introduced and eventually gained acceptance in England.

Whether for war or honor, personal combat has been as much a subject of fashion as efficiency. Rules for deciding which weapon to use and under what conditions a man might defend himself are influenced by status, teachers, personal experience, and a willingness to experiment. Even national pride and international trends affect how men decide to kill one another in single combat.

Sixteenth-century England magnificently demonstrates this idea. Persons of means were statutorily obliged to have armor and arms in case of a national emergency, but all classes of men were familiar with the use of the English sword. For close combat, at least to mid-sixteenth century, every Englishman desired a sword: a weapon with a heavy blade, usually pointed, always with two edges; a weapon intended for cutting or slashing, and heavy enough to cut off an arm or a leg. The English sword was used and respected for its fearsome efficiency.

The great English sword had been praised in epics and sung of in ballads; it had been the weapon of choice in war and peace for centuries. It was, as Sir Richard Burton said with more than a dollop of romantic hindsight, "not only the Queen of Weapons, but the weapon paramount between man and man" (xiv). Until the end of the fifteenth century and the advent of firearms, the history of English warfare had been written primarily by the two-edged sword. Sir Thomas Elyot in *The Governour* could say even as late as the mid-sixteenth century that sword and battleaxe training were most appropriate for the gentleman preparing for war.

The technique of medieval sword fighting was hardly subtle. The winner was usually the biggest and strongest knight who could continue pressing the attack, an attack consisting almost exclusively of slashing, smashing blows. This was the time of the two-handed or the hand-and-a-half (bastard) swords. (The two-hand sword, due to its enormous length, required an extra-long grip for both hands. The hand-and-a-half sword was shorter, though still heavy, and had a grip that could accommodate a one- or two-hand swinging style.) Great strength and endurance, not skill, was praised.

It is easy to see why early English sword technique lacked much imagination. Early medieval fighters wore mail, eventually replaced by approximately 1400 with plate armor, and the only effective way, in either case, to down a similarly outfitted opponent was by getting in enough good edge blows to knock him senseless. The opponent could then be dispatched with a special pointed weapon through slits in the visor or chinks in the armor.

Fighting in the Middle Ages was a specialty of knights and those of the upper class, requiring enormous financial expenditures to keep and use the required armor, shield, sword , horse, and retainers. For the peasant without armor, forced to defend his home or to participate in massed combat, there was less glory and more certainty of death or injury. Facing an early English sword, wielded by an armored knight, was a terrifying reality in combat well into the fifteenth century. However, by the following century, as pike and arquebus began to supplant the sword, and as gunpowder made armor irrelevant, battlefield practice took on a much different character. This was the beginning of European massed army warfare.

At the same time, between 1490 and 1550, vast quantities of arms were produced. By the reign of Elizabeth I, in peace as well as war, even the common man had access to swords, and it was well he did. Free Englishmen went armed out of necessity, for these were violent times. Joyce Youings states that acts of planned murder were far outnumbered in all countries of this period "by killings resulting directly from personal quarrels between fellow workers, fellow-drinkers and even players at games" (222). The rapidly increasing urban population (London doubled in size from 100,000 to 200,000 between 1580 and 1600) only exacerbated the violence. It is easy for us to romanticize the excitement and color of the Elizabethan age without remembering how narrow were the London streets, how dark were country roads, and how erratic and uncertain was the force of justice against criminals and lowlifes.

Thieves, cutpurses, and scoundrels were constantly on the prowl. A sword was often a lifesaver, whether rusty heirloom handed down for generations or stout sword and buckler purchased at almost any haberdasher (Aylward, *The English Master of Arms* 17). Holinshed (1586) wrote: "seldom shall you see one of my countrymen above eighteen or twenty years old go without a dagger at least at his back or side. . . . Our nobility wear commonly swords or rapiers with these daggers, as doth every common serving man also" (Aylward, *The English Master of Arms* 17).

Weapons were normally removed for masques and private entertainments and inside taverns, but they were always within reach of the owner or his apprentice, who himself frequently carried a dagger (Clark 190). Swords were worn in the streets and in the countryside. This was, after all, still a time in which a man might be involuntarily "pressed" into military service or challenged to a duel. Even field laborers at work leaned their trusty swords against a nearby tree, in case of trouble.

J. R. Hale puts it quite thoroughly when he says:

> In a period of quick tempers, volatile social and political forces, urban riots, especially in cities with large numbers of unemployed, or of unmarried, non-property-owning apprentices, could easily swamp law-enforcement officials: the civic guard and the constable and watchmen of parishes. The urban calendar was punctuated with holidays—Shrove Tuesday, Midsummer Day, Christmas—traditionally associated with punch-ups in taverns, jeering attacks on brothels or houses of unpopular ambassadors or alien communities, and roaming street gangs of hooligans whooping and smashing windows. . . . In the case of London, or Paris, it was above all riot, with the possibility in times of food scarcity of its escalating into insurrection, that was the chief motive [for possession of arms in households]. (*War and Society in Renaissance Europe, 1450–1620* 205–6)

In a violent age, self-defense became a part of everyday thinking. It was better policy to fight first and explain to the authorities later. In 1598, Shakespeare along with Will Kemp and Burbage's sons, Richard and Cuthbert, decided to move from Shoreditch to a less expensive site at South Bank. They discovered, however, that the old landlord expected to keep the building on their Shoreditch location. So on Christmas holiday, with swords close at hand should the landlord appear, they dismantled Burbage's Theatre for transport to the new site (Holmes, *Elizabethan London* 19).

The institution of a standing army by Henry VIII had somewhat lessened the need for military readiness on the part of the citizenry, but even through Elizabeth's time, martial sports of all kinds were quite popular and were encouraged by the authorities. Young men frequently practiced archery on the way to and from church services, which may account for its mention in the sermons of the time as a God-given practice that would help keep the English strong (Smythe li). Military parades, training, and practice were very common and functioned as a sort of militia preparation for the citizens. For upper class gentlemen, there was practice in the tiltyard.

Private schools of fencing, typically middle-class phenomena, could be found almost anywhere and will be described in more detail in the next chapter. Additionally, although few remain, numerous books and pamphlets on fencing were written and distributed in England before the end of the century. As early as 1545, Ascham in his *Toxophilus* could write: "For of fence in everie towne there is not only Maisters to teache it, with his Provostes, Usshers, Scholers and other names of Arte and Schole, but there hath not fayled also which have diligently and well-favourably written it, and is set oute in Printe that everie man may rede it" (Aylward, *The English Master of Arms* 18). In addition, many Italian, Spanish, French, and German fencing manuals found their way to the eager English sword specialists who could read them.

Various areas in and around London became famous for the martial activities they held. A fencer might be found playing at Ely Place in Holborn, the Belle Savage on Ludgate Hill, the Curtain in Holywell, Grey Friars within Newgate, the Bull in Bishopsgate Street, Bridewell, the Artillery Gardens, Leaden Hall, and, in particular, Smithfield, "the original site of the earlier jousts and tournaments" (Sieveking 390). Swordplay at these places often included the use of cudgels and small shields and was quite a rough and tumble affair, resulting in bruises, broken bones, and cracked skulls.

Playing the prize (from which we get the modern term prize-fight), like bearbaiting and boar hunting, is thought a typically Elizabethan pastime. A young fencer, after due application to the local English Masters of Defense, would be asked to show his skills in front of a crowd as a way of earning his own certification. He was expected to fight all the Masters within a certain jurisdiction and with a variety of weapons. Given the fact that these bouts were done consecutively over two or three days, the tests must have been brutal, requiring endurance as well as skill. We know these were very popular shows and often occurred on theatre stages. They were paid for by the applicant who was expected to pass the hat between bouts. With so much fighting in the streets and taverns and so many demonstrations of skill in the theatre occurring on such a regular basis, it has often been assumed that Shakespeare's audiences were knowledgeable and critical about quality swordplay.

For the man of breeding, sword practice was a status symbol, and expertise in swordplay was considered one of the gentlemanly arts. As Brailsford has stated, "In its form, in its demands upon skill, deftness and courage, it satisfied the more superficial requirements of the courtly tradition" (29). Sir Philip Sidney, in a letter to his brother, "Sweet Robin," urges him to "practice the single sword, and then with the dagger, let no day pass without an hour or two such exercise" (Sieveking 394). Dallington advised young gentlemen when traveling abroad to study fencing, and to allow two crowns a month for lessons—a considerable sum at a time when good beer went for a penny a quart (Hole 63). In Bass's proposal for an academy for the education of Queen Elizabeth's wards and the youth of nobility and gentlemen, he suggests a long list of studies which included, along with horsemanship, dancing, literature, and philosophy, the arts of "the Sworde and targat [a type of shield], the gripe of the dagger, the battaile axe and the pike" to be taught by a Master of Defense (Bass 7).

Royal entertainment often involved demonstrations of martial ability, including swordplay. At Saint George's feast in the third year of Elizabeth, Henry Machyn saw such a show: "The sam day at after-none was a great . . . played a-for the Quen('s) grace with all the masters [of fence;] and serten chalengers dyd chalenge all men, whatsumever they be, with mores pyke, longe sword, and . . . basterdsword, and sword and bokeler [a small shield], and sword and dager, [and] crosse [quarter] staff , . . . and odur weapons; and the next day they played agayne" (Nichols 250).

In addition to self-defense and recreation, a weapon in the sixteenth century could make a fashion statement, "as much a part of every man's dress as his coat or his shoes" (Clark 188–89). As swords were worn more frequently for street wear, this soon became an end in itself. Decorative hilts and scabbards, admired as much for decoration as protection, became the rage for a certain kind of gentleman who never had any need to fight. In his *Anatomie of Abuses,* Stubbes disparaged "the richness of hilts and scabbards" (Dillon 133). A. V. B. Norman points out that an often-overlooked element in many portraits of this period—from which we can glean many details about rapier design variations—is a sword worn at the side or held in the hand of the subject (*The Rapier and Small-sword*). Eventually, in the seventeenth and eighteenth centuries, such weapons were only fashion accessories, often ornately and expensively decorated, but worn by men who frequently had no idea how to use them. Still, in Elizabeth's time, there was an urgent need to carry a serviceable weapon, in addition to having the training and courage to use it.

It is important to note here, not only in regard to its widespread use, but also in anticipation of more technical points covered later, that the terms "sword " and "rapier" refer to two kinds of personal weapons that are constructed from interchangeable parts: the blade and the handle/hilt. Furthermore, there is nothing inviolate about a particular blade and the hilt it may be paired with. One advantage to sword blades is their interchangeability. Owners frequently replaced original, worn-out or undesirable blades with ones that were sharper, shorter, longer, or fancier. To a certain degree, it would be possible to fit a rapier blade to a sword hilt, and vice versa, though such combinations would be awkward and of only limited effectiveness in fighting. It is frequently impossible to tell if a particular blade was made to be matched with a particular hilt/handle. The reverse would be true for the handle/hilt. To speak of standard lengths or standard features in such a historical context would be misleading. The reader should assume that a wide variety of lengths, weights, and embellishments could be found in both swords and rapiers.

Our emphasis is less on the detailed differences among many weapons and more on the distinctions to be drawn between the rapier and the sword as generic weapons, each with its own techniques and development. A sword is heavy and sharp enough to be capable of cutting off an arm or leg. A rapier is designed with a much thinner blade, intended primarily for thrusting.

With all these swords at hand, personal disagreements frequently escalated into fights and duels, turning into full-blown affairs of honor that would ordinarily have ended in hurt feelings or a few bruises. In addition to the psychological factors, dueling also fed on a number of male-dominated historical and social traditions, many derived from the Continent. The duel *alla macchia*—held at an out-of-the-way spot, with no rules and no judges—was to become an annoying and distinct threat to social order and harmony by the seventeenth century.

Previously, and in sharp contrast to the *duello alla macchia,* the judicial duel of the Middle Ages had been a useful part of a centuries-old chivalric tradition in England. The judicial duel sanctioned personal combat as an embodiment of much higher values than personal glory or gain. As an honored, even mythic, institution within English medieval culture, it utilized the oversight of judges, the approval of authorities, and, ostensibly, the will of God: "With the sword, the highest Order/ That God has created and ordained,/The Order of chivalry/Which must be without wickedness" (Gies 79).

The sword had not only been used to slay criminals, it was also a symbol of knighthood, idealism, and the highest authority. This lore of the sword was still an accepted part of the culture in late sixteenth century England when other medieval signs of status—certain manners of dressing and living, wearing armor, carrying a sword—had disappeared. The emerging gentleman's code of honor which swept Europe in this century incorporated this ancient veneration of the sword and made it part of a new, more personal code of honor, expressed in the rising phenomenon of dueling with a new kind of weapon: the rapier.

Although England was initially slow in adopting the idea, for a nobility in "need of some new distinguishing mark for the [upper] class" dueling was a useful element of the new code of honor and had an irresistible appeal to many men (Kelso 96–97). Derived from well-developed Italian and French models, by the seventeenth century this often-complex code exerted a strong hold on many Englishmen. For example, Sir William Segar, in *The Book of Honor and Armes (1590),* relied on this English fascination with swordsmen and honor by mixing myth with history. In addition to detailing arcane points of heraldry and upper-class ceremonial behavior, this work included the famous "giving the lie" sequence that most likely was the basis for Touchstone's speech in *As You Like It* on the seven causes of a quarrel.

Henry VIII, for personal as well as political motivations, had encouraged the practice of arms and things military. But by the time of Elizabeth, drawing swords to settle personal disagreements was such a serious problem that laws were developed not only to ban dueling (erratically enforced), but even to regulate the length of sword blades worn in the city of London. James I condemned dueling in his *Proclamation against Private Challenges and Combats* in 1613, and his attorney general, Bacon, vowed to enforce an end to the practice (Baldick 65). These repressive measures only drove it underground. Covert dueling remained largely undiminished in scope, outlasting the sword and surviving well into the age of the pistol.

Works like Segar's recalled the romance and structure of earlier times. But dueling in the Middle Ages had been a matter for trained knights. Aggravated by the ease of procuring swords, the growing popularity of the rapier style, and an ineffectiveness on the part of the authorities in controlling such matters, by the late sixteenth century personal combat and personal honor substituted for earlier trial by combat between duly-selected knights. The way was open for uncontrolled violence. Though they continually heard it castigated in periodicals, denounced from the pulpit, and outlawed by the authorities, reading and hearing about famous sword duels became a popular pastime for the Elizabethans. The sixteenth century—often called the golden age of arms—became the "most quarrelsome" in history (Hutton, *The Sword and the Centuries* 75).

In addition to legal efforts which, like Prohibition, served only to intensify interest in the new weaponry, the scientific analysis of combat principles also attracted a growing number of fencing specialists. Prior to the Elizabethans, Englishmen were used to hacking away at opponents and simply enduring the physical strain and pain of combat in order to win. The English sword was lethal, not subtle, and "more reliance was evidently placed on agility and 'inspiration' than on settled principles" (Castle 3). But the rise of interest in the rapier demanded a completely new approach to fighting—a more studied one—resulting in new techniques and theories of defense that were based in greater measure on well-formed tactics and strategy.

The European masters of defense, Di Grassi and Saviolo among them, applied the Renaissance notion of scientific analysis to personal combat. Elizabethan Englishmen—ready to discard the old ways of fighting and to learn even more deadly techniques—were attracted to such experts. There was a hunger and a need for the kinds of principles and "secrets" the masters were about to introduce. Most teachers of defense, for commercial as well as theoretical reasons, emphasized this mystique of a secret science.

Rapier fighters acquired a deadly reputation, and by 1600 rapier teachers were in great demand. A fencing master, especially Italian or French, was almost a necessity for every gentleman wishing to learn the new ways. Fencing schools—traditionally the home of lowlifes and places of bad reputation, currying the interest of young toughs—acquired a new respectability. Who a person had studied with and what style he practiced were subjects of great interest to many men. There was a certain cachet and distinction to using exotic Italian or Spanish terms and in flourishing a new sword from the Continent. Looking back on it all with an ironic eye from the nineteenth century, Richard Burton observed: "In England swordsmanship is, and ever was, an exotic; like the sentiment, as opposed to the knowledge, of Art, it is the property of the few, not of the many; and being rare, is somewhat 'un-English'" (Burton xv).

Into this growing and rapidly changing state of fight techniques, a shifting political and social climate, and the development of newer, more deadly weapons, the fencing masters now enter with a flourish to teach us what they know.

Methods and Practice of

Elizabethan Swordplay

I

The Elizabethan
Fencing Masters

THE ASCENDENCY of the ra-
pier and rapier-dagger over the English sword-and-buckler play
reached its apotheosis during the last quarter of the sixteenth
century, a period roughly bracketed by the observed supernovas
of 1572 and 1604. This period also encompasses the careers of the
three most influential Italian fencing masters working in Elizabethan England: Rocco Bonetti, Jeronimo, and Vincentio Saviolo.
Contrarily, it marks the final decline of the organization known as
the English Masters of Defense, and all the bourgeois values they
defended.

There are many conflicting theories about the origin of the
rapier . A great deal of the controversy derives from many authors
coming to the debate, each from a certain style of fence, and each
finding that his heritage is the grandfather or alpha style. The
Germans maintain that they originated it. The Italians claim that
the Germans stole it from them. The French, Spanish, and even
the English make equivalent self-serving pronouncements.[1]

Before we explore the history of the Elizabethan fencing
masters, we must first describe the tradition of dueling. Like
the origin of the rapier, many cultures claim to be the birthplace
of dueling. Settling disputes by combat had been an accepted
practice since ancient times. Examples of this kind go back to
David and Goliath. John Selden recounts in *The Duello* that the
ancient Romans used "champions" as representatives of the
entire army to settle a war with the Alba Longa. Livy, in his
History of Rome, writes of Roman use of "proxies" to settle
combat in Spain. Tacitus notes the practice among the ancient
Celts. Plutarch, in his *Lives,* mentions it several times. As a
method of avoiding much larger, bloodier battles, dueling
between opposing favorites was an accepted tradition as late as
the middle sixteenth century. Hapsburg Emperor Charles V

I

made war on France after challenging Francis I to meet him personally, "sword in hand," on the neutral island of Bidassoa to settle their differences.

The sanctified trial by ordeal (of combat) was made law by King Gundwald (or Gundobald) of Burgundy in A.D. 501. By the seventh century the Lombards had fixed the system of judicial trial by combat, based on the idea that the truth of a case would be decided by God, since He would not allow a just man to lose. A good example of this kind of trial is Bolingbroke's challenge of Mowbray in Shakespeare's *Richard II*. Bolingbroke attempts to gain political power by accusing Mowbray of treason, with his defeat standing as ultimate proof. As late as 1571 in England, the trial by combat was still administered and endorsed by the law.

Any man suddenly finding himself committed to a trial by combat might naturally seek out professional instruction to maximize his chances of victory. On the Continent, such teachers were known as free-fighters or free-lancers. In England, fencing schools were both training grounds and hiring halls for *pugils* (called *ferrailleurs* in France and *bravi* in Italy; another translation is fencing attorney). A pugil was a proxy who could be hired to stand in for an appellant in a trial by combat. For example, a woman accused of adultery might designate a male relative to uphold her honor in the trial. Soon, any litigant whose fighting skills were lacking might hire a substitute. This system was quickly abused by notorious duelists, who believed, like Machiavelli, that the results justified the method. Such men could commit a wrongful act, secure in the knowledge that if challenged, they could maintain their innocence by killing the accuser in fight.[2] Aylward in *The English Master of Arms* recounts the story of Elias Pugin in 1220, who perjured himself in a case, confident that he could prove his innocence in the lists, but who ultimately forfeited his foot for his perjury (10).

The judicial duel evolved into the medieval joust and quickly devolved to the private duel. The use of the duel to settle private disputes, *before* coming to law, was already epidemic in many European countries by the sixteenth century. As the duel became more popular, so too did the fencing master.

A Short History of the Fencing Master

The fencing master and his school for defense can be traced at least to the Roman *lanestae* who taught in the *ludi* (gladiatorial fencing schools). The most famous of these was located in Ravenna. Flavius Vegetius Renatus speaks of the Roman soldier's "practiced" sword style (emphasizing the thrust rather than the cut) in the fourth century A.D.

Until gunpowder made armor obsolete (beginning with its use as early as the French defeat at the battle of Crecy in 1346), training in arms had two distinct branches. The upper classes, who could afford armor and the other equipment of knightly combat, felt no need of outside instruction, preferring to train within their own class. When two armored knights engaged each other the victory usually went to the larger, more sturdy combatant with more endurance. It was thought that God granted victory to the just; therefore, to the medieval mind, no amount of study would change God's will, especially since that study would necessarily be with a fencing master whose social standing was on a par with jugglers, actors, and other vagabonds.[3]

The lower classes, who fought not only on the battlefield, but in the alleys and pubs without benefit of armor, had always relied on the instruction of veteran *escrimeurs*.[4] These schools rapidly became havens and training/hiring halls for assassins, strong-arm thieves, and other unsavory characters. Their "method" likely consisted of various effective dirty tricks, especially disarms, seizures, and wrestling moves. Since the target or shield had always been the best affordable defense to the yeoman, it is likely that sword and buckler play was handed down as part of these martial techniques in England. Castle even names the *escrimeurs* as the forefathers of rapier play, since they developed and favored the *estoc*, a long, sturdy pointed sword, square or triangular in section for thrusting through the chinks of upper class mail or plate armor (22). Whichever class the prospective duelist, and whatever the social rank of his instructor, fencing schools experienced an explosion in popularity when men realized that without armor, and man-to-man, the sword was the great equalizer, recognizing neither rank nor privilege.

Gutenberg's movable-type printing in 1450 facilitated a growing circulation of fencing books—in addition to those on the duello— to feed an ever-expanding demand. Castle points out that fencing teachers probably had widespread reputations before they wrote their books (35). Nonetheless, he lists more than five hundred works published between 1516 and 1884. From the publication dates of these manuals we can trace the rise and fall in popularity of the fencing masters over three and a half centuries.

In the following sections, we examine the influence of the fencing master and rapier-dagger fence in each of the major European countries. We also note a parallel development and cross-fertilization among the major players in this field, all leading to the flowering of rapier fence in Elizabethan England.[5]

Germany

In Germany, associations of fencing teachers can be traced back to the fourteenth century. The earliest *fecht-gilde* or fight-guild, known as the *Marxbruders* legitimized itself by issuing a charter in 1480, but its members were almost certainly active long before. The oldest German fencing manual is ascribed to Hannes Lichtenawer and was published in 1389. Better known is Tallhoffer's *Fechtbuch,* containing pictures but no text, compiled in 1443.

Angelo credits the Germans with inventing the foil, meaning at that time any rebated practice weapon.[6] He says that they wanted the thrill and challenge of dueling, but not the bloodletting. So they began a movement to develop fencing as a sport. They devised blunted practice weapons and were the first to utilize an official to supervise the contests. The official would declare a winner after observing the bout for an allotted period of time.

From the German sword traditions comes the custom of clasping right (sword) hands together as a gesture of peace and goodwill. The Germans also made popular the swearing of oaths "on the sword." A gentleman offered a lady his right arm because his sword was attached at his left hip, where it might be in her way. A German's sword represented his freedom; losing the sword meant loss of freedom, and a prisoner had his sword returned when he was freed. A man's coat to this day buttons left-over-right, so that a duelist might unbutton it with his left (unarmed) hand.

Frederick III granted the *Marxbruders* letters of patent in 1480, allowing them absolute control of the right to teach fencing. However, as would later occur in Elizabethan England, a rival organization vied for influence and steadily gained popularity, eventually overwhelming the *Marxbruders* by teaching the Italian rapier play over the use of the *schwerdt* (sword). Castle notes that the *Federfechter*—as the rival group was known—ultimately (by 1590) forced the *Marxbruders* to give up the old cutting fight for the new pointing play (30).

Edwin Emerson in *German Swordplay* lists Hans Lebkomers's 1530 *Der Alten Fechter Angangliche Kunst,* with illustrations by Albrecht Durer, as the first printed fencing book in Germany (65). The most influential early German rapier manual was Jacob Meyer's *Kunst der Fechtens,* published in 1570. Castle and others point out the remarkable similarities between Meyer's book and Viggiani's book published in 1575 in Italy, after the author's death. Viggiani's school in Venice enjoyed its greatest popularity from 1555 to 1563, and Castle even suggests that Meyer, along with many *freifechters* (free-fighters) came from Germany to Viggiani's school, taking his teachings (and perhaps his manuscript) back with them (Castle 75–76).

Germany's idea of fencing as a sport was not embraced by the other principal countries (Italy, France, Spain, and England) until much later. In those countries, even when it was outlawed, dueling maintained its hold on the gentry as an effective means of settling affairs of honor for centuries to come.

Spain

Numerous authors assert that Spain was the mother of rapier fight. Sir Frederick Pollock places the birth of the rapier in Spain, holding that the ancient Roman schools and traditions remained there after the collapse of the Roman Empire. He points out that the oldest surviving rapiers are Spanish (the term rapier is thought to have originated with the Spanish *espada ropera* in the late fifteenth century), and he mentions several early Spanish fencing

manuals from around 1474. J. Palfry Alpar claims the Spanish were
the first to open fencing schools, and he cites the first book on
fencing as written by Diego de Valera in the second half of the
fifteenth century (9). In addition, at that time a Spanish group
corresponding to the *Marxbruders* was the *Arte Palestrinae* (Hale,
"The Military Education of the Officer Class" 235).

The first influential Spanish book on fencing we can trace was
Carranza's *De La Philosophia de las Armas,* published in Lisbon in
1569. The manual was well known in England at the time, though
apparently not in English translation. Soon thereafter, Carranza's
most famous pupil, Don Luis Pacheco de Narvaez, became the
favorite Spanish fight master, especially in England. His book
Libro de las Grandezas de la Espada appeared around 1600. Ben
Jonson, John Fletcher, and Philip Massinger all refer to it extensively in their plays. Jonson, in *The New Inn* (II, v, 87–88), speaks
of Narvaez: "Don Lewis of Madrid, is the sole master now of the
world!" He later describes the Spanish school (II, v, 91–92): "He
does it all, by lines, and angles, colonel. By parallels, and sections,
has his diagrams." (See chapter 3 for a more detailed explanation
of the Spanish style as the Elizabethans knew it.)

France

Documents surviving from 1292 note taxes levied on seven fencing
masters teaching in Paris (Rondelle 1). Henri II outlawed dueling
in 1547 after the death of one of his favorite courtiers, La Chastaignerie. Though illegal, the popularity of dueling was not dimin-
ished. Government edicts of 1554 ban fencing schools from the
city. But astonishingly, in the two decades of the turning of the
century (1590–1610), in France alone, one-third of the nobility—
around 4,000 men—were killed in private combats. Aldo Nadi
estimates 2,000 dead from fencing in the scant eight years between
1601 and 1609 (19).

The situation in England, especially after the succession of James
I in 1603, was probably comparable.[7] As Thornbury notes in *Shakespeare's England:* "Dead men, with holes in their breasts, were
often found by the watchmen, with their pale faces resting on door
steps of merchant's houses, or propped up and still bleeding, hid

away in church porches" (182). And in Beaumont and Fletcher's
The Nice Valour, a character hopes to save the lives of one hundred
gentlemen a month by publishing a treatise against dueling.

France's first fencing manual appears to have been published in
1568 by J. Descors, and Barbasetti tells us that Meyer's book from
Germany (thought to be a copy of Viggiani's manuscript, published posthumously in 1575) was available to the elite in France at
this time (226). Around 1570 the French monarch recognized the
first association of French fencing masters as the Academie
d'Armes.[8] In 1573 Sainct Didier (called the father of modern fencing) published his still-famous *Traicte contenant les secrets du premier livre sur l'espee seule, mere de toutes armes . . . redige par art,
ordre et pratique.*

As in Germany and England, the associated fencing masters of
sixteenth century France were jealous of their monopoly and were
especially hostile to Italian fencing masters and their style of play.
In the famous duel between La Chastaignerie and Sieur de Jarnac
that prompted Henri II to ban dueling, Jarnac used a hamstring
cut taught to him by Caizo, a pupil of Achille Marozzo (see Italy,
below). In 1619, Vincent Vamarelli, who had a letter of patent
from the Queen Mother Maria de Medici to teach fencing, refused
to undergo the certification process of the French Academy. He
was forced by law to close his school. On the whole, the French
masters learned the lesson their English counterparts missed and
were much more effective at banding together to keep out foreign
teachers of fence.

Italy

In Italy, the first fencing manual we can trace dates from 1410. *Flos
Duellatorium* by Fiore di Liberi is similar to Talhoffer's *Fechtbuch*,
with illustrations showing knights assaulting one another. In 1528
Castiglione published *The Courtier* in Venice, noting that the
qualities of an ideal courtier should include a knowledge of wrestling and all weapons on foot.

Achille Marozzo was considered the father of the sixteenth
century Italian fencing masters. His *Opera Nova* was popular
enough to sell out three editions between 1536 and 1615. Marozzo

continued an old tradition of distinguished Bolognese fencing schools, taking over from his master Antonio de Lucha.[9]

In 1553 Camillo Agrippa, the noted Milanese architect, published his *Treatise on the Science of Arms With a Philosophical Dialogue,* with illustrations thought to have been provided by his friend Michelangelo. Aylward claims that Agrippa's book had reached the English court before Di Grassi's work was translated in 1594, though of course only those courtiers reading Italian or employing Italian tutors/translators (like Essex) could have made use of it. His "scientific" inquiry into the rapier revealed the efficacy of the thrust, rather than the cut, as the basis of all rapier-fight systems and schools. Agrippa is said to have discovered the "disengage" (moving the blade from a line of engagement, where it is blocked by the opponent, to an open line of attack) by studying the bobbing head movements of fighting cocks.

Also at this time there were the noted fencing masters/authors Manciolino (also a Bolognese, whose book was published in 1531), Francesco Altoni in Florence (1550), Marc Antonio Pagano in Naples (1553), and Giacomo Di Grassi, whose work, published in Venice in 1570, had the honor of being the first of the phenomenally popular Italian books "Englished" in 1594.

England

John Marston expressed the Elizabethan esteem for the fencing master in *The Mountebank's Masque:* "A Master of Arms is more honorable than a Master of Arts, for good fighting came before good writing" (Aylward, *The English Master of Arms* v).

Even as far back as Edward I's reign (1272–1307), there had been English fencing masters teaching in the larger cities. English fencing masters had usually been commoners, not noblemen. By the end of the thirteenth century, fencing schools were of such bad character that the king was forced to take action. In 1281, and again in 1310, fencing schools were banned from the city of London, and other repressive measures were taken to control "brawlers."

Aside from the swashbuckling (a term derived from the sounds shields and bucklers make when clashing) of the exuberant younger students in the streets, there was the more serious problem of the pugils who hired themselves out as proxies in trial by combat. Criminals were often allowed to appeal one another, that is, escape their sentence by implicating someone else in the crime. The appealed party could challenge his accuser. As noted before, a skilled fencer could swear false evidence in a case, secure in the knowledge that he could prove it upon the body of any who said him nay. It quickly became profitable for the pugils to defend an innocent accused by an apprehended criminal trying to save his own neck.

Repressive legislation failed to dim the popularity of the fencing schools. The city of London's records show that when a scholar wished to "play his prize" for admission into the Guild, so great were the crowds that most businesses in the city shut down for the day. The continued use of pugils to settle disputes both in and out of court may have been a contributing factor in the widespread adoption of trial by jury instead of trial by combat.

Aylward claims that there was already an association of fencing masters by the mid-fifteenth century, but that a "guild could not lawfully fulfill its essential function of control over a trade or calling unless it had received the warrant of a representative body of citizens, and also paid its ferme to the king" (*The English Master of Arms* 16). Since legally they were not allowed to keep schools of fence in the city, their association as masters must have been clandestine.

In 1540 Henry VIII granted letters of patent to the Masters of the Noble Science of Defence (hereafter called the English Masters), who had organized, like the *Marxbruders* to prevent unauthorized (read competing) fencing schools from succeeding. In 1545 Roger Ascham noted in his *Toxophilus* that "of fence, all most in every town there is not only Masters to teach it, with his Provosts, Ushers and Scholars, and other names of art and school, but there hath not failed also which hath diligently and favouredly written it, and is set out in print, that every man may read it" (Sieveking 389).

It was an era of immense social, scientific, and economic upheaval. Europe was almost constantly at war. Rome had been sacked in 1527, shattering the Papal state. Spain's empire was threat-

ening to engulf England itself, and there was the exploration/
exploitation of the New World. *Hamlet* echoes the mood of the
period in its dark, obsessive concern with things internal, with
politics and madness, with revenge and power. In one thirty-year
period—from 1530 to 1560—the state religion of England changed
four times. Henry VII brought an English Catholicism, Edward
VI's advisors turned the country towards Protestantism, Mary was
nicknamed Bloody Mary for returning the country to Catholicism,
and Elizabeth brought a return to Protestantism. It was in this
turbulent context that the rapier was first brought to England.

Dillon claims that Rowland Yorke introduced rapier play into
England around 1587 on his return from fighting for the Spanish
in the Low Countries (132). Mercutio's "Spanish blades" in *Romeo
and Juliet* refers to the then newfangled rapier (I, iv, 84). But
certainly the rapier was known before this date. There are references to the rapier in official government papers as early as 1540.

Stow's *Annals* (1631) fixes the heyday of the rapier between 1570
and 1580 at the earliest. He notes that around 1560 "the ancient
English fight of sword and buckler was only had in use" (Aylward,
The English Master of Arms 17). However, soon after, in the twelfth
or thirteenth year of Elizabeth's reign (1570 or 1571) "began the
long tucks and long rapiers, and he was held the greatest gallant
that had the deepest ruff and the longest Rapier. The offence to
the eye of one, and the hurt that came . . . by the other caused
Her Majesty to make proclamation against them both, and to place
selected grave citizens at every gate, to cut the ruffs and break the
Rapier's points of all passengers that exceeded a yard in length of
their rapiers, and a nail of a yard in depth of their ruffs" (Morsberger 13). The rise in popularity of the rapier from this time until
well into the turn of the century (around 1605) is easily traced.

The swift emergence of the rapier, and the Italianate ideas it
represented, mirrors England's move in three short decades from
a late medieval culture to the cultural heritage of the early Renaissance. From the defeat of the Spanish Armada in 1588 to the
ascension of James I in 1603, in fencing, as in almost all other areas,
England absorbed a century's development from Spain, France,
perhaps Germany, and especially Italy. These dates match the

introduction of the Italian masters (Bonetti, Jeronimo, and Saviolo) and the fall of the English Masters of Defense.

Douglas Russell encapsulates the feel of the time: "Art moved from unity, balance, and logic to personal invention, self-conscious stylization, and bizarre fantasy. The result was ambiguous, unsettling, elegant, precious, and complex—anything but logical, natural, and simple" (114). For example, books on manners were more popular than fencing books.[10] Russell notes one manual from 1581 detailing stylistic differences between various countries. Northern Europeans were described as heavier, weightier, and less animated in movement and gesture. The people of the Mediterranean (especially the Italians) were seen as "hot": moving, speaking, fighting quicker. To the English, almost everything Italian, especially the new deadly (and fashionable) rapier was fast and immensely desirable.

Fencing lore to this day pairs nationalities with certain weapon types. In competitive fencing, the Teutons were thought to excel in sabre technique because of their rather squat, square, powerful torso shape. The French were said to be masters of the foil, partly because they tended to be small of stature. The Italians, particularly northern Italians were held to have an almost genetic predisposition to the epee, which is particularly suited to a tall and thin body shape. Sir Richard Burton claimed this myth explained the northern European (especially English) fondness for heavy cutting weapons, and that the slightly built southern Europeans (especially Italians) naturally evolved a thrusting swordplay because they could not match the northern European muscular style (xix).

The translation into English of Castiglione's *The Courtier* had an enormous impact. From it the English ruling class derived much of its ideal of the soldier/poet/scientist/statesman. The Renaissance idea that man could improve himself by study caught on like wildfire, and men like Sir Walter Raleigh, the poet Sir Thomas Wyatt, and Elizabeth's favorite, the Earl of Essex, set the examples. Benvenuto Cellini was admired as much for his fencing as for his art. Pope Paul III explained away "Benito's" killings by saying, "Men unique in their professions, like Benvenuto, were not subject to the laws" (Lacey Smith 308).

Gentry who lacked training in personal combat were seen as
deficient and as uncouth as those who lacked knowledge of the
social graces. This keen interest in the fencing school and the
fencing manual, together with the scientific nature of the inquiry,
led those at the forefront to Italy and the new rapier-fight of
Agrippa, Marozzo, Viggiani, and Di Grassi. This attraction for
"the white arm" (Burton's romantic term for any bladed weapon
for personal combat) continues among educated men to this day.
Aldo Nadi, in his 1943 *On Fencing,* asserts:

> Only a narrow mind could doubt fencing is an art. True artists
> recognize and admire other arts besides their own, and I have
> yet to find one, be he musician, sculptor, painter, writer or
> actor, who does not succumb to the galvanic attraction of
> fencing as soon as he or she grasps its full meaning. The
> greater the artist, the greater his ever-increasing passion for
> it. Perhaps this is so because all arts are interwoven into one.
> I shall never forget the thrill I experienced in Paris several
> years ago on seeing the headline of an article in the *Paris-Soir*
> bearing the signature of one of the most distinguished French
> music critics. It read: *Toscanini, the fencer.* (15).

By 1583, in order to gain his Master's Prize William Mathewes
had to include the rapier and dagger in his weapons of proficiency, along with sword and buckler, the longsword and
backsword. Even the English Masters of Defense had finally—
reluctantly—acknowledged the passion Englishmen had for the
rapier.

1550–1605: The Italian Invasion

The story of the thirty years' war between the English Masters of
Defense and the Italian teachers Rocco Bonetti, Jeronimo, and
Vincentio Saviolo really begins in the reign of Henry VIII. In
the 1530s Henry had strengthened the nation's defense by heavy
investment in foreign mercenary units, reviving the Winchester
Statute of 1285 (stipulating the weapons, armor, and other gear the
gentry were required to keep in readiness), and ordering huge
amounts of the most current weapons (especially firearms) and
armor from Italy and France. Wisely, he had also imported armor-

ˑers, swordsmiths, and gunsmiths in an attempt to start a national armaments industry of his own. In 1522 he held a national dooms-day survey detailing the wealth and arms supplies of all his subjects. Fearing a French invasion, in 1539 Henry placed a massive foreign arms order.[11] Just one year later, he granted the disgruntled English Masters of Defense their letters of patent to further encourage local military preparation.

Aylward lists Ric. Beste (a gunner in the Tower of London), eight other masters, and eleven provosts as the charter members (*The English Master of Arms* 19). They created four ranks: scholar, free scholar, provost and master. All the original and subsequent members were required to take an oath not to teach their art to thieves, murderers, and other undesirables. They fixed the prices for instruction, decided that no newly made master could open a school within one year of attaining that rank, and fixed the requirements for upgrading status. For example, to pass from scholar to free scholar, a fee was required and a private test of proficiency had to be passed by defeating six free scholars at several different weapons. Then the scholar might play his public prize, which could involve considerable expense but promised fame and possible profit, since audiences threw money to their favorites. A minimum of seven years of study was required before application for provost could be made, then additional private and public prizes had to be passed. The provost then apprenticed for seven more years before playing his Master's Prize, a highly popular public event.

The Masters, like actors, tended to gather in the districts just outside the city limits, in Bishopsgate, Holborn, Ludgate Hill, Newgate, and especially Blackfriars (which enjoyed exemption from city regulations because it had been a monastery). Theatres and taverns in these districts were the favored places to hold prize fights.

On Henry's death in 1547, the warrant he had issued was invali-dated. Warrants and patents (such as Elizabeth granting Raleigh the monopoly of licenses to sell wine in 1583) were the prerogative of the new monarch, to be doled out to supporters in the new regime. The English Masters tried in vain to have their imprimatur restored over the next three reigns.

The Masters enjoyed rising popularity with their sword-and-buckler style and their prize fights. In 1565, after a famous prior attempt, John Blinkinsopps won his free scholar prize in a fight at Pye Corner. His examination must have been as popular a diversion in his day as is a heavyweight title bout today. Ben Jonson refers to him as "Blinkinsopps the Bold" in *The New Inn*.

Rocco Bonetti first came to England in 1569, a turbulent time. Mary Stuart had fled to Scotland, tensions with Spain were mounting, Netherlands was in prewar unrest, the violence in Ireland continued, and Cosimo de Medici ruled Tuscany with the endorsement of Pope Pius V, who excommunicated Elizabeth. Just three years earlier a jealous Lord Darnley, Mary's husband, and his compatriot Lord Ruthven had stormed into Holyrood House and dragged David Rizzio (a singer in the royal quartet) away from Mary and murdered him with fifty-six thrusts of sword and dagger. Scarcely eleven months later, Mary had Lord Darnley and his house blown to bits. The Spanish ambassador in London was plotting with the Catholics and providing intelligence to his sovereign, Philip II. He was, in turn, watched closely by Elizabeth's courtiers.

Aylward tells us that Bonetti was a soldier of fortune and a secret emissary from Catherine de Medici (then regent of France) to spy out Elizabeth's attitude toward a proposed marriage to the Duc D'Anjou, who became Henri III. In Spain, Carranza had just published his enormously influential *De La Filosofia De Las Armas*. Bonetti married an Englishwoman (complicating his citizenship status) in 1571, but he left shortly for further adventures, including a campaign in Antwerp in 1574. He returned in 1575 to find his wife dead (we do not know the cause) and his English property appropriated by his wife's relatives, Robert Burbage and John Vavasour.

Though tragic for Bonetti, the years of absence had been good ones for the English fencing master. In 1571 Henry Nailor, an English Master, was appointed as champion for a defendant in a civil suit. The appellant never appeared for the duel.[12] In 1573, William Mucklow, an original member of the English Masters of Defense, ordered the keeping of a Book of Minutes for the organization. Their record continues through 1589.

In 1573, because of his financial straits, Bonetti had agreed to carry letters between the French ambassadors in London and Edinburgh. Bonetti had the letters copied and sent to Chief Secretary of State Walsingham. Walsingham showed his gratitude by interceding for Bonetti in the matter of his wife's property.

John Lyly had the lease on some rooms in Blackfriars where William Joyner, another original member of the English Masters, had a school.[13] In 1576 Bonetti bought the lease from Lyly and by imputation from Lyly's patron, Edward De Vere (the Earl of Oxford). Bonetti then opened his famous fencing school. He was just what the gentry were looking for, with their new-found interest in the rapier and all things Italian. Fortunately, Bonetti was several social steps above the English Masters, yet still comfortably below the gentlemen who frequented his salon. Silver tells us, "He caused to fairly drawn and set round his school all the Noblemen's and Gentlemen's arms who were his scholars, and hanging right under their arms their rapiers, daggers, gloves of mail and gauntlets" (Aylward, *The English Master of Arms* 41). He also provided luxurious furnishings, a writing desk with stationary for the use of his students, as well as a clock with a large dial.

Bonetti's teachings and his growing popularity cannot be separated from the huge interest in the *code duello*. Half of Saviolo's book is devoted to quarrels and their causes. Selden's book in 1610 is devoted solely to its history. George Walter Thornbury reminds us, "Sir Andrew's duel, Benedick's challenge, and Mercutio's death, were *daily* incidents of a period when the duello was a science" (36). Bonetti's school surely benefitted from these popular ideas of the duel.

The English Masters, distressed at Bonetti's success, sent emissaries to him offering to arrange the date when he could challenge them for his Master's prize. Bonetti declined on the grounds of class, refusing to recognize mere fencers, which Francis Bacon had termed "but an ignoble trade" (Aylward, *The English Master of Arms* 43). Their dislike of him included the middle-class distrust of most things Italian (and especially Catholic). Only four years earlier Norfolk had been executed for plotting Elizabeth's overthrow with Roberto di Ridolfi, a Florentine banker in London. At one point some of the provosts (Aylward identifies two as Isaac

Kennard and Francis Calvert) apparently tried to provoke Bonetti into drawing as he went about his business in the city (*The English Master of Arms* 44).

It has been suggested that some men in the employ of the Earl of Oxford were pursuing Bonetti as well. Linda McCollum writes that Oxford hated Bonetti, possibly because Lyly had leased him the Blackfriars rooms without the earl's consent, and that "Oxford's men were often in trouble for causing frays . . . such noted swordsmen as Sir Roger Williams (the prototype of Fluellen in *King Henry V*), 'Denys the Frenchman' (Captain Maurice Denys who wrote under the pen name of John Soothern), George Gascoigne (the poet and soldier adventurer) and Rowland Yorke (his receiver who is credited with introducing into England the practice of foining [thrusting] with a rapier in dueling)" (14).

Both groups wanted to dispatch Bonetti in a street brawl, a provocation he was careful to avoid. According to the code of honor, it wasn't difficult to have the choice of weapon in an impromptu quarrel. One simply "gave the lie," as in Segar's example. "Simon meeting with Lewes saith, 'Draw thy weapon, and I will presently prove thee a liar and a Varlet: Or if thou wilt not draw, then art thou a Varlet also'" (Morsberger 55). In *Romeo and Juliet* even the serving men are savvy enough to inquire "is the law of our side if I say Aye?" before their challenge, "draw if you be men" (I, i, 45–46, 59).

In 1578 Bonetti used his contacts on Elizabeth's Privy Council to intercede for him with the lord mayor of London, because he was regularly being accosted by the fencers of the city. In July of 1579 the council directed that the mayor imprison the offenders named by Bonetti.

By 1581, the international situation became even more tense, with rumors of plots and counter-plots. The Spanish ambassador reported to Philip, "if even so much as a cat moved the whole edifice would crumble down in three days" (Lacey Smith 237).

The English Masters apparently realized the need for obtaining court patronage, as Bonetti had, and in 1582 the Earl of Warwick petitioned for his servant John David to play his provost prize. The next year Blinkinsopps the Bold and Anthony Ffenreuther were "allowed" Master. As the political climate worsened, so did the reputation of the Masters. In 1583 English Master John Duel was involved in a bizarre marriage scandal, and later he was killed by one of his own students. In the same year, Walsingham extracted yet another assassination plot from Francis Throckmorton by torture.

The incidents of personal and political violence only grew worse. In 1584 William of Orange (William the Silent) was assassinated by Balthazar Gerard under orders from Philip II. Doctor William Parry, a member of Parliament, plotted to assassinate Elizabeth, supposedly with a bullet blessed by the Pope. At this time Bonetti's lease on the Blackfriars salon expired, and he had some trouble getting the landlord to renew the lease, since he had remodeled the rooms extensively but was behind on the payments. Bonetti asked his patrons, Sir Walter Raleigh, Sir John Worth, and Lord Peregrin Willoughby (one of the queen's best swordsmen), to intercede on his behalf.

In 1586 Holinshed noted, "Seldom shall you see one of my countrymen above eighteen or twenty years old go without a dagger at least at his back or side. . . . Our nobility wear commonly swords or rapiers with these daggers, as doth every common serving man also" (Aylward, *The English Master of Arms* 17). That year also saw the indefatigable Walsingham uncover the Babington plot, followed by swift condemnation of Mary and her accomplices.

In 1587, the year of Mary's execution, Bonetti died. Jeronimo, who Silver called "Signior Rocco, his boy," apparently kept the school open. Whether Jeronimo was Bonetti's son, or merely his assistant is not known. That year Shakespeare's famous comedian Richard Tarleton studied with the English Master Naylor. Tarleton played his Master's Prize successfully that year, as did playwright Robert Greene. Ben Jonson mentions Jeronimo in *The New Inn* as "Hieronimo . . . the Italian that played with Abbot Anthony i' the Fryers [Blackfriars] and Blinkinsopps the bold" (II, v, 82–83).

That summer (1588) was the high-water mark of Elizabeth's reign, and the defeat of the Spanish Armada made Englishmen feel almost omnipotent. It made the reputations of Sir Francis Drake (the Dragon) and his Sea Dogs. The medieval world, repre-

sented by the lumbering military folly and feudal tactics of the
Armada, had been consigned to oblivion by modern, progressive
Englishmen like Drake, Raleigh, and Essex. In the next decade,
their fame would eclipse even Elizabeth's.

Vincentio Saviolo, arguably the most influential fencing teacher
of the time, joined Jeronimo at the school in 1590. Sir William
Segar's influential work, *The Book of Honor and Armes,* was published that same year. It may be that Jeronimo and Saviolo did not
teach at the Blackfriars for much longer. The evidence shows that
in 1593 Thomas Bruskett had the lease.[14] It was about this time
that Saviolo gained the powerful patronage of Robert Deveraux,
the Earl of Essex, who had replaced Raleigh as Elizabeth's favorite.
John Florio was Deveraux's Italian tutor, and in 1603 he would
give England its first translations of Montaigne's essays. In 1591
Florio described Saviolo (Master V. S.) in his *Second Fruites* as
"that Italian that looks like Mars himself. . . . He will hit any man,
be it with thrust or stoccata, with an imbroccada or a charging
blow, with the right or reverse blow, be it with the edge, with the
back, or with the flat, even as it liketh him."

For the next couple of years Jeronimo and Saviolo exploited the
immense English interest in rapier-fight, traveling around the country propagating their "foining fence" and enraging the English Masters. George Silver and his brother Toby challenged the Italians to
fight at the Belle Sauvage, across from Blackfriars. The Italians refused, to the public disgrace of the Silvers, who had already printed
and distributed posters and handbills advertising the fight.

Playwright Christopher Marlowe had earlier been charged with
manslaughter in the death of William Bradley in a rapier and dagger
duel involving Marlowe's friend Thomas Watson. In 1593, Marlowe
was himself killed under peculiar circumstances in a Deptford tavern
brawl.

Aylward notes in *The English Master of Arms* that by 1595 the time
was ripe for Saviolo to publish (57). Di Grassi's book, *His True Arte
of Defence,* had been translated into English the year before, possibly
by Jeronimo. Manuals by Marozzo, Agrippa, Viggiani, and Carranza were available to those who could read them in the original.
John Wolfe bought the rights to publish "a book intituled Vincentio
Saviolo/ his Practice/in two books/The first intreating of the use

of the rapier/and Dagger/The Second, of Honor and honorable/ Quarrels." Soon after, in 1596, James Burbage acquired the lease on the fencing school and used it as part of the Blackfriars Theatre. His partners at that time were John Hemmings, Henry Condell, William Sly, and William Shakespeare , who had just written *King John* and *The Merchant of Venice*.

Two years later, in 1598, Ben Jonson was living at Blackfriars. In addition to penning his most famous play, *Every Man in His Humor,* Jonson killed one of his actors (Gabriel Spencer) with his rapier in a duel at Shoreditch, but not before Spencer wounded Jonson in the arm. In 1599 John Day killed playwright Henry Porter in a rapier duel. Swordplay had become an everyday occurrence, in the streets, in the theaters, in print.

What happens to Saviolo in this period is unclear. In 1599 George Silver published his *Paradoxes of Defence,* and says Saviolo is dead. Whether from disease or as the result of a duel we are not told. But, since Silver details the deaths of Bonetti and Jeronimo at the hands of stout English duelists, we can assume from his omission that Saviolo at least did not share their fate. With Saviolo's passing we mark the high tide of the rapier and the almost total ebbing of the English Masters. Just a few years later, in 1603 when James I ascended the throne, any warrant the English Masters had claimed was invalidated. James accepted French fencing masters from Henri IV to teach the Prince of Wales. The next year English Master John Turner acquired his reputation for putting out the eyes of his opponents, which would earn him assassination in 1612. In 1605 Silver wrote an "addendum" to the *Paradoxes;* after arguing so forcefully against the new weapon in that earlier work, his *Bref Instructions* now contained notes on the rapier.

Even the English Masters of Defense had reluctantly acknowledged the passion Englishmen had for the rapier by 1583. That year, in order to gain his Master's Prize William Mathewes included the rapier and dagger in his weapons of proficiency, along with sword and buckler, the longsword, and the backsword. Scarcely twenty-five years later the fashion among fencers would shift to France and the new style. The transition rapier or small sword, then became the rage, evolving into today's modern fencing style.

Di Grafsi his true Arte of Defence,
plainlie teaching by infallable Demonſtrations,
apt Figures and perfect Rules the manner and
forme how a man without other Teacher or
Maſter may fafelie handle all fortes of
Weapons afwell offenſiue as defenſiue:
VVith a Treatiſe
Of Difceit or Falsinge : And with a waie or
meane by priuate Induſtrie to obtaine
Strength, Iudgement and
Actiuitie.

Firſt written in Italian by the fore-
faid Author, And Engliſhed by
I.G.gentleman.

Printed at London for I.I. and are to be fold
wi hin Temple Barre at the Signe of
the Hand and Starre
1594.

The true Art of Defence exactlie

teachinge the manner how to handle weapons safelie, alwel offensiue as defen-
siue, With a Treatise of Disceit or Falsing,
And with a mean or waie how a man
may practise of himselfe to gett
Strength, Iudgement,
and Actiuitie.

T Here is no doubt but that
the Honorable exercise of
the Weapon is made right
perfect by meanes of two
thinges, to witt : Iudgment
and Force : Because by the
one, we know the manner
and time to handle the we-
pon (how, or whatsoeuer occasion serueth:) And
by the other we haue power to execute therewith, in due time with aduauntage.

And because, the knowledge of the manner
and Time to strike and defende, dooth of it selfe
teach vs the skil how to reason and dispute thereof onely, and the end and scope of this Art con-
sisteth not in reasoning, but in dooinge : Therefore to him that is desierous to proue so cunning in this Art, as is needfull, It is requisite not
onelie that he be able to iudg, but also that he be
stronge and actiue to put in execution all that
which his iudgement comprehendeth and seeth.
And this may not bee done without strength and
actiuitie of bodie : The which if happelie it bee

A 1.   feeble

2

The Beginning
of the Italian Invasion:
Giacomo Di Grassi's
True Arte

GIACOMO DI GRASSI'S *His True Arte of Defence,* published at the very end of the sixteenth century, is the earliest fencing manual in English that has survived. Information about English fencing styles before the arrival of Di Grassi and other European fencing masters is tantalizing but limited. For instance, Roger Ascham in a passage of *Toxophilus,* dated 1545, states that not only could masters and scholars of defense be found throughout England, but the secrets of their art were "set outye in Printe that everie man may rede it" (Sieveking 389). Such writings would be invaluable today, but no such works remain.

No biographical information about Di Grassi is known. The original Italian edition of the manual, *Ragione di adoprar sicuramente l'Arme si da offesa come da difesa; con un trattato dell' inganno, et con un modo di essercitarsi da se stesso, per acquistare forza, giudicio et prestezza,* was published in Venice in 1570—about the time that Camillo Agrippa and Achille Marozzo were also distributing their works on swordplay. Di Grassi's treatise became the basis of a work by Henry de Sainct Didier in 1573, and many of his principles were later imitated by Meyer and Sutor in Germany (Castle 49).

His True Arte was translated and published in English in 1594 by "I. G. Gentleman." The English edition is a fairly accurate translation of Di Grassi's earlier treatise and includes crude copies of the Italian edition's illustrations (Jackson vi). Carl Thimm suggests that "I. G." is Jeronimo, either the son or top apprentice of Rocco Bonetti, a controversial Italian fencing master, who was suspected of being a spy in the employ of Catherine de Medici and the Italian court (121). However, as Aylward points out, Jeronimo reportedly was killed in a fatal duel before that year (*The English Master of Arms* 57). So the exact history of the manuscript, including who translated it, remains unclear, although we do know that Thomas Churchyard was the English editor.

Di Grassi simplified what Agrippa had devised, adding his own refinements. For instance, he reduced the number of guards to three and appears to be the first to have divided the sword blade into various parts. Castle says that Di Grassi's concern for a blade's sense of touch in parrying is remarkable for its time (49). Di Grassi's manual also criticizes the then-common practice of indiscriminately parrying with both false and right edges of the blade, a practice that had existed for centuries, according to Hutton (*Old Sword-Play* 24). Di Grassi demonstrates that parries with the false (thumb side) edge are mechanically weaker. Most notably, his manual was first to emphasize strongly the importance of thrusts (point) over cuts (edge), even with the English sword. Arthur Wise suggests that "if we can regard Agrippa as the originator of the Rapier, then we might regard Grassi as the precursor of the small sword of the eighteenth century" (*The Art and History of Personal Combat* 40).

Di Grassi claims to have written down the master keys to fencing, not just another book of fencing techniques. This in itself makes his manual different from many of those that came before. His sole purpose is to reveal the underlying principles and practices of "this Art, and reduce the confused and infinite number of blows into a compendious sum and certain order: The which principles being but few, and therefore easy to be known and born away, without doubt in small time, and little travail, will open a most large entrance to the understanding of all which is contained in this Art" (Jackson 7).

Di Grassi's teaching was elegant and simple. His intent was to break down swordplay, particularly the new Italian rapier style, into logical units—a scientific approach. Elizabethan fencers encountering it for the first time must have been dazzled, for *His True Arte* taught a vastly new and different technique. Even more compelling are the many examples of techniques applied to real combat situations. The manual sounds as if it were written by a practiced swordsman, not an armchair theorist.

In the Dedication, the English editor Thomas Churchyard refers to the "knowledge of Arms and Weapons, which defends life, country, and honor" and thus is a most fitting subject for the author's pen and for the glory of his lord (Jackson 3). Personal combat is placed in the context of a higher, collective good, not individual glory or violent instincts—an approach common to much fight literature, not only of the Elizabethan age, but of most ages. Optimistically, Churchyard states:

> The fine book of riding hath made many good horsemen: and this book of Fencing will save many men's lives, or put common quarrels out of use because the danger is death if ignorant people procure a combat. Here is nothing set down or speech used, but for the preservation of life and honor of man: most orderly rules, & noble observations, interlaced with wise counsel & excellent good words, penned from a fountain of knowledge and flowing wit, where the reasons run as freely as clear water comes from a Spring or Conduit. (Jackson 4)

It would have been impossible to have sold the merits of fencing technique to a society already uneasy about the proliferation of weapons in all classes (particularly in the lower ones) without referring to noble causes, patriotism, and honor. Consequently, fight training began to develop a cachet which made it appealing without being politically provocative.

A fencing school may have distributed *His True Arte* as a way to attract new students. Reading the manual could only whet the appetite of the novice, who might then enroll. In "To the Reader," Di Grassi adds he felt a duty to pass on to others what he had found only by intense work and study. From childhood he "delighted in the handling of weapons," and after having "spent much time in the exercise thereof, was desirous to see and behold the most excellent and expert masters of this Art" (Jackson 6).

But to his dismay, Di Grassi discovered that such a variety of approaches only made fighting more confusing. He could deduce no order or rule from all these teachers, only personal tricks and idiosyncrasies. There were too many variations to be subsumed under a logical structure; some fight styles seemed more wishful thinking than sound teaching. Eventually, after long study and serious thought, he was able to overcome the chaos of teachings and formulate his theory of personal combat.

He then sets out his manual's organization. Starting with the fundamental principles on which his technique is based, he proceeds from simple to more complex variations. Di Grassi reminds the reader that he will not resort to mysterious language, seeking rather a simplicity in his descriptions. For this reason he asks that we proceed slowly and carefully, since much matter will be phrased in few words.

Many fencing masters felt the need to clothe their work in some more respectable light, and Di Grassi is no exception. As we discussed in chapter 1, fencing masters were caught in a compromising position. On one hand, they were delighted with the fast-growing popularity of their art. At the same time, they realized that such knowledge could easily be held directly responsible for unlawful or rebellious acts of violence. In addition to the previously mentioned "Dedication," a cautionary "To the Reader" ends with a reminder that the art of fencing, being a "principal member of the *Military Profession* . . . ought not to be exercised in Brawls and Frays . . . but as honorable Knights, ought to reserve themselves, & exercise it for the advantage of their Country, the honor of women, and conquering of Hosts and armies" (Jackson 8). For his own protection, Di Grassi places this caveat prominently in the manual.

The translator, in an appended note to the reader, points out that wherever Di Grassi has used the Italian term for "sword," the word "rapier" has been inserted. Recognizing that the English sword and buckler remained in common use among the lower classes, he says that the rapier is "more usual for Gentlemen's wearing, and fittest for causes of offense and defense" (Jackson 9). He also notes the popularity of rapier play in Italy. Such a translating decision would have been made only because the rapier was already well-established in England. Aside from making the fencing manual more contemporaneous, such a shrewd technique attempts to skew the work and help popularize the new rapier ways.[1]

In addition, I. G. reminds the reader that since these principles are so wise and scientific, they equally apply to English sword fighting. In a nudge at hostile English fencing masters, the translator concludes that "no wise man of an impartial judgment, and of what profession soever, but will confess himself in courtesy far indebted both to the Author and Translator of this so necessary a Treatise" (Jackson 10).

His True Arte of Defense states that superior swordplay is based on judgment and force. Judgment means clear theory and sound techniques, using the appropriate technique in the right situation for maximum effectiveness. Force is the physical capacity to carry out a judgment; it is muscular strength, balance, timing, and coordination.

Judgment and force are intimately related and function synchronously. A fencer may know many techniques and be well-versed in theory, but not have the physical skill to carry out his ideas in combat. Likewise, over the long term, great skill—God-given or trained—will not in itself carry the day:

> Therefore let every man that is desirous to practice this Art, endeavor himself to get strength and agility of body, assuring himself, that judgment without this activity and force, availeth little or nothing: Yea, happily giveth occasion of hurt and spoil. For men being blinded in their own judgments and presuming thereon, because they know how, and what they ought to do, give many times the onset and enterprise, but yet, never perform it in act. (Jackson 14)

Di Grassi reminds his readers that the new rapier fighting is of a different nature than earlier swordplay. A knight's greatest asset was his brute force and the stamina to apply it until the opponent was defeated; force, in other words, might have worked in the past. But a rapier fighter needs a much more sophisticated blend of physical technique and mental discipline.

The five principles—called Advertisements—that follow are his basic theoretical truths for all fighting and thus are foundations to all true judgment—something analogous to Oriental martial arts basing their systems on natural movements in animals, for instance. Di Grassi says that though a particular fencer may not have learned these principles, if he is successful in combat it necessarily follows

he was using them, albeit unknowingly. But how much better if
he knows them and follows them always! The Advertisements are:

1. Since a line is shorter than an arc, it follows that a strike
(thrust) in a straight line is faster than a cut.

2. "He that is nearest, hitteth soonest." That is, if you see your
opponent drawing back or raising his sword, you should attack at
that moment. A corollary states that the sword should be kept in
front of the body and poised to strike at all times. This is an
important distinction, prefiguring the modern "on-guard." We
should remember that, in Di Grassi's day, swords were of widely
varying lengths, from thirty-six to sixty inches, or more. The fencer
with the longer sword has an instant advantage, as Hamlet's first
query reveals: "These foils have all a length?" (V, ii, 254).

3. There is more force at the extreme circumference of a circle
than close to the center; that is, a cut (or "blow," as Di Grassi
says) with a sword is more effective toward the point than toward
the hilt. Analogous to the modern notion of "point of percussion,"
it means that every sword has a spot which combines the most
speed with the most force when used to cut. This would not,
however, be the area closest to the tip.

4. "A man may more safely withstand a small than a great force"
(Jackson 16). In other words, and incorporating number 3, when
parrying, move into the hilt (center of the circle/small force) rather
than to the tip (circumference of the circle/great force).

5. Every movement of the sword and body takes place in a
certain amount of time and has a rhythm.

To say that any movement takes place over time strikes us as ridic-
ulously self-evident. In Di Grassi's day, however, the whole idea of
breaking down an attack into such isolated concepts was startlingly
new, mirroring the growing Renaissance interest in scientific inquiry. This is the first of a number of insights he presents that
changed the thinking of swordsmen, making swordfight survival
dependent on something more than brute chance. Before the end
of the sixteenth century, such notions had not been taught in any
noteworthy way in England (and only marginally in Italian, French,
and Spanish manuals). As is the case even in our own day, more
thought was given to the development of new weaponry than to
how that weaponry would actually function in combat.

There has always been a tendency to analyze combat—like most physical activity—in general terms, from a metaperspective. The literature of warfare and combat, until quite recently in fact, is full of vast movements of men and richly suggestive theories about how best to overcome a vague thing called the enemy. Most theorists assume a hypothetical maximally effective gunner or pikeman or bowman, for instance. The enormous cost in human life was a given; rarely was there much thought to reducing that cost through better psychological and physical preparation for the individual soldier.[2]

English sword fighting up to the sixteenth century was considered a "grit your teeth and bear it" sort of affair. Wielding an English sword or greatsword required considerable strength and physical stamina. But the rapier changed all that, to the great dismay and jealousy of the English Masters of Defense who had been so successful with the old methods (see Silver). To the traditional English fencing master, the rapier was so foreign, so *Italianate;* now strength had to be tempered with accuracy and speed.

Psychologically, the act of fighting is intense and quick. When life or death hangs in the balance, the sense of time quickens and perception falters. Up to the sixteenth century no one had thought it possible to analyze a fight which might take only seconds to complete, or that anything other than luck or natural ability could save a man. But Di Grassi suggests that such activities can be analyzed and that fundamental qualities of speed, balance, and efficient use of the body and mind may be influenced by training, rather than left to chance. Understanding fight psychology and behavior was a necessity as more and more men wore swords at their side and the popularity of dueling grew. This shift in theory and training through the work of men like Di Grassi cannot be overestimated.

Di Grassi says that a skilled fencer will fight efficiently, using only the number of strikes required to vanquish an opponent. In addition, the whole notion of falsing and slips—feints—is an advanced skill that can work only if used selectively. Feints cannot be used as substitutes for good technique because a trained opponent won't go for feints and an untrained one simply won't recognize them as feints, which defeats their purpose.

Keeping the five principles in mind, we can now begin a review of Di Grassi's teaching.

Of the Sword

Admitting that almost any object can be thrown or held to advantage and may be termed a weapon, Di Grassi says that he will concentrate on the one that is "more honorable, more usual . . . [and] more safe": the rapier (Jackson 19).

Visualizing the shoulder as the center, when delivering an edge blow (his term for cut) the arm's length then forms the radius of a circle (see Figure 1). Moving through this circle takes time to complete, too much time for Di Grassi. Recognizing the beginning of an opponent's edge blow, a well-trained swordsman may advantageously strike with a thrust. Therefore Di Grassi does not recommend circular attacks. He prefers to utilize thrusts, relying on the inherent slowness in cutting attacks.

We should not overstate the originality of the thrust technique for the Elizabethans. Certainly it was used even by armored knights. Some early medieval swords were rounded at the tip, but many more had sharp points. However, the preferred attack with swords was always the more aggressive cut. Di Grassi, with all the rapier specialists, showed that the thinner-bladed weapon's greatest advantage lay in the projection of the point (see Figure 2).

Regarding the thrust, the fencer must consider the distance to target and his own body position relative to the sword. It is advantageous to go directly into the thrust, utilizing the length of the sword already present, rather than spending time retracting the sword and then launching the thrust. The pictures in Di Grassi's manual indicate that fencers in his time were quite close, much closer than in our day (see figures 3 and 4).

Di Grassi divides the sword into four parts. "For as much as the effects which proceed from the length of the sword are not in every part thereof equal or of like force [then I will] name . . . each part, to the end every man may understand which are the parts of the length wherewith he ought to strike, and which the parts, wherewith he must defend" (Jackson 21).

The third and fourth parts (the front half of the sword to the

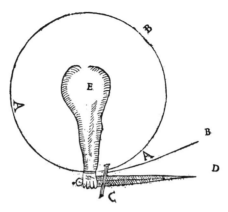

Figure 1. A demonstration from Di Grassi comparing cuts (as an arc of the circle with the shoulder at circle's center) and thrusts (C to D). (By permission of the Folger Shakespeare Library)

Figure 2. The fighter on the left is prepared to deliver a quick thrust. The fighter on the right has two options for starting an attack with sword held high: a direct edge blow or a thrust. However, the thrust requires more time. (By permission of the Folger Shakespeare Library)

Figure 3. Di Grassi's high ward and low ward demonstrated. Note the relative closeness of the figures and the deliberate use of the empty hand for protection. (By permission of the Folger Shakespeare Library)

Figure 4. A demonstration from Di Grassi of rapier and dagger. Again, note how close the figures are; a simple extension of the blade and slight step forward with the front foot constitute a thrust. Also note the blade lengths and construction of the hilts. (By permission of the Folger Shakespeare Library)

point) are best for striking in a cutting motion. This is because a sword cut is swiftest—has a greater impact velocity—at the tip (the circumference of its circle) rather than close to the grip or center. The first and second parts of the blade (from the middle of the blade back to the hilt) are best for warding (parrying) the opponent's blade, due to their proximity to the handgrip. Di Grassi does not exclude cutting attacks, but he does emphasize thrusts as more efficient.

The fencer's arm extends the sword's cutting power, and from this we can derive the best sword cuts. A wrist cut is swift, but not so strong, while the force coming from the shoulder is stronger, but not so swift. Therefore, when delivering an edge blow (cut), Di Grassi recommends not using the shoulder so much. Here we must remember that Di Grassi means a small cut that would cause a slashing wound in the face or arm (in modern terms, a saber cut), not a cut that would take a man's arm off. Instead, "he shall only use the compass of the elbow and the wrist: which, as they be most swift, so are they strong enough, if they be orderly handled" (Jackson 23). Therefore, a good fencer using sound technique will not raise the entire arm above the head, thus exposing himself to a quick thrust from the defender. Di Grassi says that the best cutting motion will tend to stay in front of the fencer's body, providing protection and quicker response time.

His next point is a bit cluttered in reasoning, but boils down to this: both cutting and thrusting motions are based on circular or partially circular movements. This is because human joint move-ment is always circular. In a cutting motion, both the sword and the arm obviously carry in an arc. Surprisingly, close observation of a thrusting motion reveals that the arm arcs slightly up or down—depending on whether the fencer is starting from low ward (guard) or high ward—while the point of the sword arcs in the opposite direction in order to keep going forward.

For example, if the sword is held in a low ward or guard, arm extended down and a bit to the outside right, with the point aimed at the opponent, to thrust the arm must raise from down alongside the leg up to waist height. This is one arc. In order to keep moving forward, the point must arc slightly downward as the arm comes up. This is the second, or counter, arc. Put most simply, the arm makes a half-circle up, but the wrist makes a compensatory half-circle down; thus the movements cancel each other out and result in a straight line thrust. As Di Grassi puts it: "If therefore the arm would strike directly at the point . . . it is necessary that as much as it lifts the handle upwards, the hand/wrist moves itself circularly downward. Therefore seeing by this discourse it is manifest that the blow of the point, or a thrust, cannot be delivered by one simple motion directly made, but by two circular motions, the one of the Arm the other of the hand, I will hence forward in all this work term this blow the blow of the straight line" (Jackson 27).

A thrust is more difficult to perform with a sword (as opposed to a rapier) largely due to the size and construction of the hilt. In addition, most swords of the time had no protection for fingers placed over the hilt, and thrusting with an ordinary sword grip can be awkward. The rapier, however, allows the fighter to hook his forefinger over the *quillons* (the cross bar). In addition, that forefinger is protected by the *arms of the hilt* (rings above the *quillons* and to each side of the blade). This orientation of hand on handle and finger over *quillons* provides better mechanical control of both hilt and blade point. The mechanics of holding the weapon thus largely determine how and which attacks may be best delivered.

Footwork

Most fighting arts concern themselves at some point in training with footwork. Di Grassi says this element is indispensable in keeping safe distance as well as speed in attacks: "from them [footsteps] . . . more than any other thing springs all offense and defense" (Jackson 30). (In this, as we shall see later, he stands at odds with Silver, who maintains—in good, traditional English sword style—that the action of the hands and weapon must lead the feet.) Di Grassi is not precise in describing how large the footsteps should be, only that they be "a reasonable pace, in such sort that if he would step forward to strike, he lengthen or increase one foot [step], and if he would defend himself, he withdraw as much, without peril of falling" (Jackson 30).

The feet may move forward, backward, or diagonally in straight lines. Moving forward, for instance, the back foot may pass the front, what Di Grassi calls a whole pace (Jackson 30). This can also be done by moving slightly on the diagonal, or "crooked" pace, thus removing the fencer's body from the opponent's line of attack (Jackson 30). The whole pace may also be used to retreat.

A half pace is defined, for example, as drawing the rear foot up to the forward foot, or when, starting from a feet-together position, stepping forward with one foot (Jackson 31). A half pace may also allow the fencer to retreat, moving one foot backward and leaving the other foot in place. This motion is similar to modern fencing technique, always leaving one foot in contact with the ground. Half paces are used in both straight and crooked passes, forward and backward (see Figure 5).

Di Grassi also incorporates circular passes which involve a delib- erate "compassing" of the forward foot in a small arc to the rear, or vice versa (Jackson 31). Compassing continually moves the body out of target and provides a balanced pivoting action, allowing easy retreat and attack. This compassing movement may have been a holdover from earlier swordplay.

Of Paces

The swordsman "must have great care to make his pace and move his hand at one time together" (Jackson 33). Leg movement should match body and hand movement. For instance, when thrusting or parrying with the sword in the right hand, the right foot position is critical: when thrusting, the foot and leg give drive to the motion of the sword; when defending, foot and leg provide a solid base for parrying. Pace also determines the length of an attack or defense.

For similar reasons, Di Grassi does not believe in feinting by waving the arm or weapon (see his Dealing with Deceits and False Blows and Thrusts below, pages 48–49). Without balanced footwork, body motion is scattered and more open to counterat- tacks. (Remember also the previous argument which demonstrates that an experienced opponent will use your feint as a time to attack, and an untrained fighter will not recognize it.) In addition, Di Grassi cautions that only in rare circumstances should both feet leave the ground. In leaping or skipping, "keep one foot always

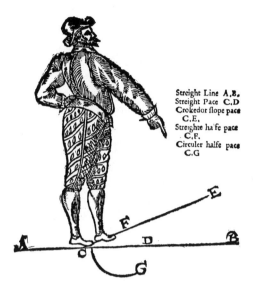

Streight Line A.B.
Streight Pace C.D
Crokedor flope pace
C.E.
Streighte ha'fe pace
C.F.
Circuler halfe pace
C.G

*Of the Agreement of the Foot
and Hand.*

Figure 5. A demonstration from Di Grassi of the straight pace (C to D with the front foot), the crooked or slope pace (C to E with the front foot), and the circular half pace (C to G). Di Grassi calls this the "Agreement" of the foot with the hand, a key difference between rapier play and the earlier English sword footwork. Following from this, the straight half pace is apparently mislabeled and should be called a crooked or slope half pace. (By permission of the Folger Shakespeare Library)

firm and steadfast: and when he would move it, to do it upon some great occasion, considering the foot ought chiefly to agree in motion with the hand, which hand, ought not in any case whatsoever happen to vary from his purpose, either in striking or defending" (Jackson 33).

Footwork and its coordination with weapon movements is stan-

dard training technique now, but it was revolutionary in Di
Grassi's time. A weapon is an extension of the fighter's power.
That power is developed through coordinated body use, so that
all movements in the body are ultimately expressed in the weapon.
The weapon and the body are parts of a whole system, and Di
Grassi insists that skill has to be developed down to the feet.

Wards

"Wards in weapons are such sites, positions or placings which
withstand the enemy's blows, and are as a shield or safeguard
against them" (Jackson 35). That is, a ward serves to close off a line
of attack. Even more importantly, wards function as preliminary
positions to attacks (Castle 37). Di Grassi's three wards are high,
low, and broad.

High ward follows from the natural position of the sword after
it is drawn from the scabbard: that is, point down or level, hilt
and hand up, and blade protecting against attacks to the head and
upper body. By raising the point forward it is possible to strike
quickly at the opponent. This is preferable to raising the point
behind in an overhead strike or cut to the opponent's face. Such
a move unnecessarily opens the fencer to a quick counter.

The broad ward for a right-handed fencer is held with hilt
slightly below the waist on the right side of the body, a few inches
out. The point still holds a line directed at the opponent, not
straying too far to the right to make the defender vulnerable to
attack. From broad ward, the fencer can parry nearly any attack
and strike quickly in a straight line.

The low ward is held just outside the front knee with the point
directed slightly in and toward the opponent. Di Grassi warns
against a low ward with weapon arm held straight out in front.
The fencer would have to withdraw the sword before striking,
thus taking too much time for the attack. "This ward therefore
must be framed with the arm stretched downwards, near the knee,
but yet on the outside thereof, because after this manner a man
stands safely, commodiously, and more ready, both to strike and
defend" (Jackson 39).

How to Strike

"Without all doubt, the thrust is to be preferred before the edge-blow, as well because it strikes in less time, as also for that in the said time, it doth more hurt" (Jackson 40). Di Grassi points out that the Romans used thrusting swords for this very reason: "thrusts, though little and weak [compared to cuts], when they enter but three fingers into the body, are wont to kill" (Jackson 40).[3]

A thrust must be performed by compassing the rear foot in line with the sword and forward leg. "And in finishing of the blow, to draw his hinder-foot a half pace forwards, and so by that means the blow is longer and stronger, and the shoulder and side are only opposite to the enemy, and so far off from him, that they may not be struck" (Jackson 40). This places more power behind the movement of the weapon. The resulting posture foreshadows the modern lunge.

There are times when a cut can be desirable. If the opponent has closed in and the sword point is off to one side, a quick cut is more effective than retracting and then thrusting. Also, if an opponent has beaten your sword aside, you can immediately follow in with a cut to his body from the position to which you have been beaten.

How to Defend

Defensive movements to meet either a cut or thrust are three. The first is the simple block with your own sword against the attacker's. Di Grassi says there are frequent errors with this technique: for instance, stepping back and thus blocking close to the opponent's sword point, where the force is greatest (Advertisement 3). Although this is a more natural or habitual action, by alternatively stepping in to the parry the fencer gives himself a close-quarters opportunity for attack.

A second parrying fault occurs after the parry. Withdrawing the feet and body allows the opponent time and opportunity for a renewed attack. To prevent this, Di Grassi recommends that when parrying, the defender step in strongly with the rear foot in a crooked pace forward, thus parrying further in on the opponent's sword. This diagonal entry preserves proper distance to allow a follow-up attack.

Another method for avoiding a cut or thrust is simply to move completely out of the way, to either side. However, since the attack is not defused by such a maneuver, an opponent may quickly follow up with another strike. For this reason, Di Grassi suggests that voiding maneuvers with the body be accompanied by some counterattack. The most notorious example was called the *passata* or *passata sotto* in which the defender voids by quickly lowering his body and simultaneously raising his sword; the surprised attacker literally runs onto the blade. The attacker's motion, much like having a chair pulled from under him as he sits, only carries him forward, out of control, through empty air. Mercutio's derogatory "Come, sir, your passado" refers to this move (*Romeo and Juliet* III, 1, 83).

Attacking from the High Ward

Quick attacks may be made from the high ward. "From the beginning to the ending of this blow, there is never any time given to the enemy to enter, by reason that the point stands always directly against him" (Jackson 48). The rear (left) foot is drawn near the right foot, then the right foot is advanced to thrust from this ward. A cutting attack is again not recommended since it takes too long for the point to reach the opponent.

If an initial thrust from high ward is parried by the opponent's sword, a follow-up with the edge in a cutting attack is expeditious. Di Grassi points out that a number of follow-ups are possible from high ward, in a series, as long as the opponent parries only to the outside. He adds that the cutting motion may be used with either the true (finger) edge or the false (thumb) edge of the blade in such an attack.

If the preceding attacks are unsuccessful and the fencer finds himself in low ward, then:

> he ought with the straight pace of the right foot, discharge a thrust *underneath*, being already prepared, the which thrust is so strong, both for the aptness thereof and increase of the pace, that it pierces through any impediment withstanding it.

And all these blows . . . being roundly delivered one after another with such swiftness as is required, are in a manner not to be warded. Besides, *they have so great increase of pace, that it is not possible for the enemy to retire so much backward, as these increase upon him forward* (emphasis added). (Jackson 50)

This final thrust was called the *stoccata,* and it is what Mercutio refers to when he says, "Alla stoccata carries it away" (*Romeo and Juliet* III, 1, 73).

Defending the High Thrust

If the opponent takes the high ward, the defender should go to low ward. As the first thrust comes in, it should be parried to the right at the same time taking a sloping pace to the left (the opponent's right). While doing so, if the point is kept down the attacker will likely run onto it, or, with a straight pace forward, the point may be thrust at the attacker.

Di Grassi's idea is an intriguing one and carries with it a central distinction between traditional sword parries and those made with the rapier: rapier parries initiate attacks. Many fighting styles use parries and attacks as two separate physical actions. But without such abrupt stops and starts, by blending parries and counterattacks as one action, the rapier fencer attains greater speed. There is no pause between defense and attack and blade action is smoother.

A related point here is that various wards, in combination with paces, develop many different angles between two fencers. This is another innovation of Di Grassi and the new fencing masters of the late sixteenth century. In Di Grassi's early fencing manual we see the rudimentary use of "lines of attack"—a thrusting attack requiring less room for execution—that eventually became the complex smallsword technique of the eighteenth century.

For high edge blows, the best defense is to take the attacker's blow out of line with the parry, then continue into him with the point. Di Grassi adds that since the edge cut will take longer to complete, a quick counter-thrust is also effective.

Attack/Defense in Broad Ward

The most obvious and effective attack from broad ward is the thrust underhand, that is, under the opponent's guard. With a slight pace forward of the front foot, an edge blow delivered "from the wrist of the hand" would also be advantageous (Jackson 52). Di Grassi seems to favor this ward above the other two because the fencer may attack, defend, or simply "watch for the enemy's coming" in relative safety (Jackson 53).

It follows then that it is best to be in broad ward to defend against attacks from the broad ward. An attack by cut is outpaced by a quick thrust or may be met by a smooth combination parry and thrust or cut. Defending against the underhand thrust is a relatively simple parry.

Attack/Defense in Low Ward

An attack from the low ward is obviously an effective technique since the sword point is already aimed at the opponent and an attack may be carried out quickly by simply raising the weapon at the same time the body steps forward. But if the opponent is similarly positioned in low ward, the attack must go outside or inside, rather than over or under, the defender's sword. The in/out attack is accomplished by judicious use of an oblique pace to either side. It may also be necessary for the attacker to lift his sword hand to keep his blade free from defending parries either left or right. Di Grassi implies that this is a tricky situation, with both fencers in a strong beginning position, and much will depend on taking the initial advantage quickly and smoothly.

From the defender's point of view, when both fencers are in low ward, a cutting attack from above or below is easily defended. The thrust, however,

> may prove very mortal and deadly. Therefore, when this thrust is given within, it must be beaten inwards with the edge of the rapier, requiring the turn of the [defender's] hand also inwards, and the compass of the hinder foot, so far towards the right side, as the hand goes towards the [enemy's] right side . . . [and] the enemy shall no sooner have delivered the thrust, and he [the defender] found the sword, but he ought

to turn his hand; and with a reverse to cut the enemy's face, carrying always his forefoot on that side where his hand goes. If the enemy's thrust comes outwards, then . . . with the turn of his [defender's] hand he beat it outwards with the edge of his sword increasing in the same instant one slope pace . . . [then following with] another straight pace, [defender] delivers a thrust already prepared. (Jackson 55)

Note again that a parry combined with a thrust is recommended. This simultaneous defense-offense is an innovation by Di Grassi.

The Rapier and Dagger

The classic rapier and dagger (also called the poniard) was the most common combination of weapons at the time of Di Grassi's writing and afforded the fencer a further compounding of attack and defense variations.[4] The Elizabethans thought that striking and defending simultaneously was possible only with rapier and dagger. As Di Grassi modestly points out, however, the reader now knows from what has already been written in the manual that this is not so. A single rapier may parry and attack as part of one motion. But he admits that the addition of the dagger gives "great help to the other" (Jackson 56).

The fencer must know, however, how to allocate various parts of the action to each weapon. The dagger covers the left side down to the knee; the sword protects the entire right side and below the left knee. Di Grassi cautions the reader that any parry on the third and fourth part of the opponent's blade—for example, if retreating from a cut instead of moving in—must be met with more than dagger since so much force has to be absorbed.

Wards with Rapier and Dagger

The dagger ordinarily is held at arm's length, the point tending toward the opponent. Di Grassi says that there are two popular ways to orient the blade when parrying: with the flat or with the edge. It was thought that initial contact in parrying would be more effective with the edge leading. Additionally, by keeping the edge facing the opponent's blade in parrying, the sword breaker style of dagger (a dagger with blade having many slits cut into it, used to grab and trap the opponent's sword blade) could be employed most effectively. Di Grassi doubts the usefulness of such techniques, but he leaves the choice up to the reader.

It is important not to parry across the vertical midline of the body; all parries should be outward. Therefore, the dagger always parries to the defender's left, the sword out to the right. To reverse these directions gives the attack much more time to hit the body. Modern stage and film fight choreographers regard this rule as fundamental to actor safety.[5]

Attacking and Defending from High Ward in Rapier and Dagger

Attacks from high ward may be initiated with either foot forward. The advantage of starting in high ward with the right foot behind is that more body force may be applied to the rapier thrust. In either case, Di Grassi suggests that the attacker finish in low ward. Edge blows are not recommended from this ward due to the defender's ability to respond with a second weapon.

There are three basic techniques to defending attacks from high ward. Starting from low ward, the defender may parry with dagger, step in a pace, and strike with the rapier from underneath. A second strategy is to ward with the sword by making contact with the attacker's blade and riding it up and out of the way, at the same time entering and thrusting with the dagger or, alternatively, continuing in with the rapier. The third way involves stepping a slope pace, finding the enemy's sword with the dagger, withdrawing the sword momentarily, and thrusting underneath the opponent's blade with a straight pace.

Attack and Defense from Broad Ward with Rapier and Dagger

The broad ward is particularly unsuited to cutting attacks. For defense, Di Grassi recommends parries out of the low ward by a slope pace, especially using the dagger. Alternatively, he points out that rapier parries should be done with the edge; immediately following, the point should be thrust at the opponent's face, at the same time taking a compass step with the back foot.

Attack and Defense from Low Ward
with Rapier and Dagger

It is from low ward that the advantage of thrust over cut is most apparent. Indeed, "it is better . . . rather to discharge thrust after thrust, than any edgeblow" (Jackson 66). The right foot may be placed forward, preparing to launch an attack, or behind, anticipating an attack from the opponent. The fencer might think that an attack launched with the weapon foot behind develops more force, but unlike attacks from high ward which can profit from this technique, the increase in traveling time for the point to hit the opponent from low ward negates that advantage and renders it only marginally effective.

Attacks may be made between the opponent's rapier and dagger, or by taking the outside line on either side. Attacks from within function with a kind of scissoring action: moving the opponent's rapier aside with the dagger and, while moving in a slope pace or straight pace (depending on distance), thrusting home. Outside lines may be initiated at the opponent's face, and when he responds by parrying outward, performing a reverse edge cut to his leg and finishing off with a thrust from above.

Another good tactic would be to fake a small edge blow (controlled from the wrist). When the opponent tries to parry, take a slope or crooked pace, lift up the sword hand, and thrust downward. A third variation is to attempt the wrist cut, feeling the opponent's parry and taking up the parry with your dagger, thereby freeing your rapier for a low or high thrust.

Di Grassi says that low ward is the most common defense for rapier and dagger. Keeping in mind that all parries are used to discover new attacks—not made simply to defend and break contact with the opponent—the picture we get of this fighting style is not the polite, elegant tit for tat that is so often reproduced in modern theatrical productions and movies. Di Grassi's is an aggressive, street-wise style that looks for any opening. No opportunity is lost to find and wound the opponent.

He is also careful to point out that when parrying thrusts, the body must be taken out of the straight line. The defender never stands in position to accept the opponent's blow or thrust. A good fencer evades attack by opening up to various angles. Di Grassi suggests that any attack can be distorted by the parry into an out-of-balance opening for the defender if speed and timing are correct.

Rapier and Cloak

Di Grassi says that the cloak was discovered as a weapon quite by accident, but its development in his system is by design. The Elizabethan cloak was commonly worn anywhere from waist to knee length. For fighting, the cloak is removed and wrapped once or twice around the forearm, leaving some length hanging. Such a wrap should never be used to defend a cut. The cloak is most valuable when hanging loose. That looseness gives the cloak its deceptive power and makes it ideal for parrying thrusts. Parries may be made to either side, being careful to keep the left leg back, or stepping by half steps, "for at these weapons, it is dangerous lest (making a whole pace) he entangles his foot or feet in the cloak and fall down therewith" (Jackson 74).

Attack and defense configurations are similar to those previously explained in the dagger section (pages 41–44), with some modifications. For example, in attacking with rapier and cloak in low ward, it may be possible to envelop the enemy's sword with the cloak, immediately following with a thrust. This would be particularly effective when entering inside (between opponent's rapier and dagger). Another technique is to throw the cloak over the opponent's head from a distance and then close quickly for the thrust. Salvator Fabris illustrates this move in his *Sienz e Practica d'Arme* (Wise, *The Art and History of Personal Combat* 84).

A variation on this is to grab an opponent quickly by his cloak and pull him down, since the cloak is collared around his neck. Flinging the cloak at an opponent, or feigning such a move, can also be effective; but actually throwing a cloak not only takes time (the air slows down the cloak's movement), it leaves the defender helpless. Di Grassi even suggests that the "cloak may be flung or thrown with the edge of the sword, when one stands at the low ward, with the point of the sword turned backwards, on the left side and the cloak upon it . . . he may take the cloak on the edge

of the sword and fling it towards the enemy, and then strike him
with . . . a blow" (Jackson 157).

When defending with the cloak, the fencer must carefully judge
how far the opponent's blade enters. The cloak is valuable only in
parrying the first section—four or five inches down the blade
from the point. This parry would be most effective if followed
immediately by a rapier thrust. Parrying a cut with the cloak can
be dangerous if the attack comes in at a high angle since the cloak
can blind the defender. But low thrusts may be easily parried as
long as the appropriate footwork—retreating and compassing—
is used.

Sword and Buckler

The buckler is a small, round shield, from six to twenty inches in
diameter, which is held with one hand in a strap. Sharp points or
hooks—sometimes as much as a foot long—were often attached
to the front center of the buckler, useful for attacking or entrapping
the enemy's blade.

The buckler's small size increased its usefulness. Unlike the older
large shield, a buckler could be quickly and easily moved to many
positions in response to an attack. It was also easy to see over or
around the buckler and thus not be blind-sided by an attack. In
addition, a buckler could be held at arm's length, providing an
irritant to the attacker's vision and offering an efficient parrying
angle closer to the source of attack (Advertisement 3).

Di Grassi recommends that the flat of the buckler face the
attacker at all times. Edge blows may be easily voided by circular
or slanted paces and turning the buckler to the opponent's blade.
Thrusts may be parried in much the same manner; indeed, if the
buckler is held at arm's length toward the attacker, thrusts seem
useless or even dangerous due to the great distance that must be
traversed by the attacker.

Defenses and attacks with buckler in low, broad, and high wards
is quite the same as with dagger or single rapier. The body is still
moved slightly out of the line of attack with a concurrent slide
into the parry and counter-thrust. Another quite effective move is
to parry with both sword and buckler against a high attack, for

instance, and then to thrust the buckler (with point) into the opponent's face, giving him what Di Grassi calls "the *Mustachio*" (Jackson 88).

In this section, Di Grassi describes another key part of his fighting theory. "He that defends has great advantage . . . he that wards by increasing, defending and drawing near unto the enemy, is so placed, that he may easily hurt him" (Jackson 91). In other words, the wise fencer will first move into the enemy (increasing). This absorbs the attacker's initial energy and sets up the defender's counterenergy. Defending involves some sort of parry and a concurrent foot movement (slope or circular pace, for instance). "Drawing near unto the enemy" is the defender's counterattack which takes place in that instant's pause at the completion of the opponent's initial attack. The great success of this technique resides in absorbing the motion of the initial attack. Many martial arts are based on this very notion; the defender can gain the advantage by drawing the attacker in a bit further and then closing.

The Square and Round Target

The target is a large shield, often used to protect the body from the neck down to the knees or below. Originally devised for use in war, it was occasionally used in personal combat. Di Grassi says that the target is generally used in two ways: resting it against the thigh and settling in behind it without moving much, or holding it pulled in against the chest.

The best defensive position for the target is lightly held away from the body, below the chin. This affords the best line of sight for the defender. It also establishes a central position from which the target may be swung left, right, up, or down. Also, the square target should be held in a triangular orientation, not square to the ground. This means that the upper point is beneath the face, the lower point is straight down, and there is a point for each side or shoulder. This opens up vision even more and establishes ready-to-use edges for parrying edge blows.

Given its large size, the target is an excellent instrument for parries and entries to the opponent's space. The variety of attacks and defenses from the various wards are similar to the previous descriptions. Attacks that arrive from inside or outside may be equally neutralized by appropriate pacing, parrying, and counter-attacking. The angles of thrusting attack in a rapier/target fight would be quite small with two experienced fencers, so even the slightest tilt or twist of the target might reveal an opening. The size and weight of this weapon also provides a reassuring defense against most edge blows.

Di Grassi adds instructions at this point regarding the round target, or what we more commonly refer to as a shield. This weapon should be held slightly to the fencer's left side, providing an unobstructed view of the opponent just over the edge, but still enough in front and away from the defender's body to offer quick protection. As with the square target, attacks and defenses may be aided by the sheer size and weight of this weapon. Shield-to-shield bashing must have been a frequent element in this kind of fighting.

The Case of Rapiers

One uncommon fighting style in Di Grassi's time used what was called the "case of rapiers," case meaning two. As Di Grassi points out in this brief section, a fencer should be able to "as well manage the left hand as the right"—a warning to the vast majority of fencers who are decidedly one-handed (Jackson 107). Such even-handed skill must include attacking and defending. There is a great temptation to attack with two swords in hand, completely forgetting wards and body evasions. However, Di Grassi feels that with the case of rapiers, as with any other set of weapons, it is better to defend with one sword and attack with the other.

Defenses and attacks with the case of rapiers develop out of high, broad, and low wards, as in other weapon combinations. Low ward continues to be the ward of choice for defense. Parries with two swords have an additional advantage: a counterattack can be mounted after either sword has parried. Sloping and circular paces increase the effectiveness of this two-sword combination; there is always a sword pointed at the enemy. Only a slight change in footwork or hand placement magnifies the motion of the point.

Di Grassi objects only to one defensive position for two-sword technique: "But I suppose no man so foolish, who handling these weapons, will suffer both his swords to be without [that is, both of the opponent's swords are between yours], being a very unsure ward whereof I leave to speak" (Jackson 115).

The Second Part
Dealing with Deceits and False Blows and Thrusts

Indiscriminately using feints (deceits) is a bad habit, according to Di Grassi. Unfortunately, fencers do sometimes succeed with a few such moves in practice and begin to believe that these moves can be relied on in real combat. Di Grassi points out that there is a fundamental difference between practice and real fighting: fencers in practice bouts never intend hurt; real combat usually ends in death. Therefore, a good fencer should perform deceits and false blows only in practice sessions, with the idea of training hand/ eye coordination:

> It is a brave and gallant thing and worthy of commendations to be skillful in the apt managing of the body, feet and hands, in moving nimbly sometimes with the hand, sometimes with the elbow, and sometimes with the shoulder, in retiring, in increasing: in lifting the body high, in bearing it low in one instant: in brief, delivering swiftly blows as well of the edge as of the point, both right and reversed, nothing regarding either time, advantage or measure, bestowing them at random every way. (Jackson 145)

Di Grassi then lists a variety of movements that may be used when playing at falsing: shifts of the feet, bearing the sword point backwards or forwards, feinting a thrust high and attacking low, and so forth. With rapier/dagger, it is usually the rapier which will feint, though he points out that the dagger can be thrown from a distance, even after parrying the opponent's sword.

Extreme falsings should be used only in extreme situations; the dagger throw cited above is one, since it leaves the defender with one less weapon. Also, pretending to throw the dagger is effective only if the enemy responds; the fencer should immediately follow such a reaction by attacking.

But to Di Grassi's way of thinking, these are borderline and dangerous measures when one's life is on the line. Such devices tend to be improvisations based on momentary developments in a fight; they are not carefully practiced techniques that can be depended on to defend the fencer's life.

Conclusion

Di Grassi's simple yet sophisticated breakdown of swordplay into lines of attack and defense, strengths and weaknesses of various weaponry, and basic fight training, must have seemed a wonderful advance to the Elizabethans. The rapier opened up exciting and dangerous possibilities; exciting for it made solid dueling techniques attainable to any man willing to practice, dangerous for it meant that death from the point of a sword could happen in an instant.

Di Grassi's genius lies in his simplification of fight principles that could be adapted to almost any situation. Through basic training methods, coupled with his five basic advertisements and weapons strategies, the fencer could "attain to that perfection in this Art which he desires" (Jackson 184).

VINCENTIO

SAVIOLO

his Practise.

In two Bookes.

The first intreating of the use of the Rapier and Dagger.

The second, of Honor and honorable Quarrels.

LONDON
Printed by Iohn Wolfe.
1 5 9 5.

VINCENTIO SAVIOLO
HIS PRACTISE.

Haue long and greatly defired (my deare friend *V.*) to learne this noble fcience, and efpecially of you, who did put the firft weapons into my hands: wherefore (feeing fo good opportunitie is fo fitly prefented) I coulde wifhe that wee might fpende this time in fome difcourfe concerning the Arte of the Rapier and Dagger, to the end that I might thereby, both the better retaine the title which I haue alreadie learned, and alfo adde fome new leffon thereunto.

V. Certes (my louing friend *L*) as wel for that I haue found you to be a man of a noble fpirite, as in regard of the great loue which I beare vnto you, as alfo to the end that hereafter when time fhall ferue, you may be better knowen vnto fundry Gentlemen my good friends, I am content to yeeld vnto your requeft, and therefore demand boldly any thing wherein you defire to bee refolued.

L. Sir, the loue which you beare mee I know to bee exceeding great, and therefore haue no doubt that you will fayle me in anie part of your promife, for the which fauour I acknowledge my felfe infinitly beholding vnto you. I fhall defire you therefore, according to your iudgement and skill, to refolue and inftruct mee in fuch
doubtes

3

Vincentio Saviolo:
His Practise in Two Bookes

GEORGE SILVER reports that Vincentio Saviolo arrived to teach in Rocco Bonetti's school in 1590, four years after its inception. Saviolo was an Italian born in Padua, but he claims to have traveled extensively throughout Europe, and his book shows him to have mastered not only his Italianate heritage of fence (heavily influenced by Marozzo, see Di Grassi's *His True Arte*), but also the Spanish (Carranza, Narvaez) and perhaps German styles.[1]

Licensed in November, 1594, Saviolo's *His Practise in Two Bookes* bears the date 1595. In it he synthesizes the best of all the schools of fence into one cohesive system.[2] It seems likely this was the style taught in Bonetti's college, since Saviolo is known to have continued instruction with Jeronimo at Bonetti's and in the provinces for at least several more years. But Saviolo's immediate fame and influence were brief. Aylward tells us in *The English Master of Arms* that by 1599, Saviolo was dead.

Vincentio Saviolo was arguably the most significant and controversial teacher of fence in England at this time, and his teachings had a profound effect throughout Elizabethan society. Many references in the literature of the time call him by name, many others allude to him and his teachings. Certainly Silver's book is a vehement attempt to refute Saviolo's techniques and their appalling (to Silver) popularity. Ben Jonson knew him, and Shakespeare cannot have failed to have been acquainted with him. Touchstone's famous comic disquisition on the "seven lies" in *As You Like It* (V, iv) is supposed by Warburton, Craig, Linda McCollum, and others to be taken from, or at least to allude to, much of Saviolo's second book, *Of Honor and Honourable Quarrels*. Likewise, many of the fencing terms in *Romeo and Juliet*, including Mercutio's description of Tybalt as "the very butcher of a silk button," are thought to refer directly to Saviolo and his teachings (II, iv, 23).

Tillyard points out in *The Elizabethan World Picture* that the

Elizabethans were obsessed with the ordering of their universe. They were convinced that the earth had already seen its Golden Age and that the end of civilization was soon approaching. They took the observed supernovas of 1572 and 1604 as support for this view. Tillyard explains, "the battle between Reason and Passion, the commonplace of every age, was peculiarly vehement in the age of Elizabeth. The theological trend of the whole sixteenth century had been Pauline, and in Paul it is this war, not contemplation or beatitude, that holds the first place" (75). In their attempts to reconcile thought and action, "The Elizabethans saw this single order under three aspects: a chain, a set of correspondences, and a dance" (Tillyard vii).

The martial dance was a particularly fascinating notion to most of the great Elizabethan minds. Jonson, Raleigh, Sidney , Porter, and Wyatt were all at least as concerned with their status within the fighting community as within the literary community. Ben Jonson killed one of his actors in a rapier-and-dagger duel in 1593. Henry Porter was killed in a rapier fight in 1599. Christopher Marlowe was a notorious duelist, and died in 1593 in a Deptford tavern fight.

Men of war in particular began to seek a new order in their profession, precipitating a fierce battle between the schools of the new rapier men and the old-style warriors.   We recall from chapter 1 the conflict between the English Masters of the Noble Science of Defense (who approached their art more as a craft than as a science), and the foreign fencing styles and teachers from the Continent (especially Italy). Silver, the prototypical English fencing master, brags of the lusty gentleman, gifted by nature, who could beat any scientific rapier man. Saviolo, representing the Italian Renaissance view that science and art supplement and improve nature replies:

> Nature may do very much to frame a man apt and fit for this exercise, both in respect of convenient courage and strength, but all these . . . are nothing except he have knowledge of art. We see that the very things themselves which are brought forth by nature good and perfect, if they be not holpen by art, by very course of nature become naught and unprofitable. As the Vine if it be not holpen by art comes to no proof nor

profit, so likewise other trees how apt soever they be to bring forth excellent fruits, if they are not husbanded grow wild and degenerate from their natural perfection. For that one having those good parts and abilities by nature before mentioned, yet not knowing them, he cannot use them to his benefit but by the means of skill and judgement; which a man by his industry and practice attains unto. Therefore they which make so small a reckoning of art, in this respect are worse than beasts. Especially those which are practised in fight, in which a man may perceive a kind of reason and art. Seek to learn it and not to scorn and despise it. Especially in such a case where so deeply concerns a mans life, that in the stirring of a foot he may be suddenly overtaken and slain. (Jackson 204)

Castle points out that "no master of fence is likely to have written a book until he had acquired a widespread reputation as a teacher" (48). From this, and from Silver's attacks on Saviolo, we can infer that Saviolo's reputation must have been great indeed by 1595. Certainly English interest in the rapier (especially Italian teachers who taught it) was still on the rise. The dire necessity for close study of the art is borne out by current statistics indicating that "premeditated murder accompanied by gross brutality was far outnumbered in all countries investigated by killings resulting directly from personal quarrels between fellow-workers, fellow-drinkers, and even players at games" (Youings 222). Shakespeare neatly encapsulated the tenor of the time in Mercutio's rebuke of Benvolio (whose name means "of good will" in Italian) in *Romeo and Juliet:* "Nay, and there were two such, we should have none shortly, for one would kill the other . . . thou wilt quarrel with a man that hath a hair more or a hair less in his beard than thou hast. Thou wilt quarrel with a man for cracking nuts, having no other reason but because thou hast hazel eyes. . . . Thou hast quarrelled with a man for coughing in the street, because he hath wakened thy dog that hath lain asleep in the sun" (III, 1, 15–20, 23–26).

Fencing books usually concentrate on the history, forms, and philosophies of the art, since it is notoriously difficult to actually learn movement arts from a book. But Saviolo continues a different tradition of fight instruction books that take the form of a dialogue,

in this case between V (Vincentio Saviolo) and Luke (the hypothetical student).[3] The first of Saviolo's two books allows the
reader to listen in on a scholar's lesson, developed step-by-step.

"Scholar" for the Elizabethan did not have its modern-day book-
ish connotation. Except for some of the young gentlemen of the
court, it is doubtful whether many of the scholars enrolled in
fencing schools of the time could read. In Saviolo's terminology,
a scholar is not merely one who studies, but a specific ranking of
a student of fence, very like today's martial arts systems that use
different colored belts denoting varying levels of skill. In the English Guild (Masters of Defense) there were two ranks, scholar
and free scholar (see chapter 1 for more details of the test and
ranking system). A prospective free scholar had to pass a private
test against six brother scholars at both long sword and backsword,
and to play a public prize against as many free scholars as chose
to meet him. Though Saviolo declined to play his prize for the
endorsement of the English Masters, it's clear that he uses the term
scholar in its English fencing context.

Saviolo's first book, *Of the Use of the Rapier and Dagger,*
follows the structure of Castiglione's enormously popular *The
Courtier.* He leavens practical lessons in swordplay with discussions of philosophy, psychology, and art. His second book, *Of
Honor and Honourable Quarrels,* was widely read and discussed
as a kind of rule book for dueling. For a comparison of Saviolo's
method with Di Grassi's and Silver's we will focus on the first
book.

Each lesson has the flavor of a transcription of a day's instruction, in which Saviolo (V) transmits his system "entire," instruct-
ing his scholar Luke (L) not only in the hows of rapier play, but
also the whys. A good example occurs very early in the first lesson
after Saviolo has satisfied Luke's query to "show me how I must
stand upon my guard, or assail mine enemy" (Jackson 210). The
master explains one of the basic tenets of his system:

> V. So I will, and as before I have told you of diversity of
> teachers and variety of wards, so in this point also must I tell
> you that men's fashions are diverse, for some set upon their
> enemies in running, and there are others which assail them
> with rage and fury after the fashion of rams, and both these

sorts of men for the most part are slain and come to misfortune
... sometimes they [these techniques] are very necessary,
according as a man finds his enemy prepared with his weapon:
but then they must be done with time and measure, when you
have got your enemy at an advantage, with great dexterity and
readiness. But as for me I will show you the wards which I
myself use, the which if you well mark and observe, you cannot
but understand the art, and withall keep your body safe from
hurt and danger. (Jackson 210)

Saviolo in general advocates lying in a "sure ward" (described
below) rather than rash, blind aggression. He advocates the deadly
counterthrust (also detailed below) executed from a stable defensive position. Apparently alarmed at the deadly efficiency of Saviolo's method, Silver astutely complained, "These Italian fencers
teach us offence not defense" (Castle 130).

Luke asks what he should do in the case of a friendly combat,
in which he would desire to merely wound his opponent, not kill
him.[4] The exchange is particularly revealing of the mindset of a
typical English fencer and of the tremendous effect Saviolo's practical fighter's insights had on changing those attitudes:

L. But I pray you of friendship tell me, if a man were to go
into the field with some friend of his whom he would be loath
to kill, should not these mandrittas [types of cuts] be good to
wound him, and not put him in danger of his life, I pray you
therefore tell me your opinion, and how a man in respect of
his honor were to use and order himself, put the case he would
not kill his friend, but would willingly save and keep him from
harm.

V. I will speak mine opinion of these things which concern a
man's life and honor. First I would with every one which is
challenged into the field, to consider that he which challenges
him does not require to fight with him as a friend, but as an
enemy, and that his is not to think any otherwise of his mind
but as full of rancor and malice towards him. Wherefore when
you find him with weapons in his hand that will needs fight
with you, although he were your friend or kinsman, take him
for an enemy, and trust him not, how great a friend or how
nigh of kin soever he be, for the inconvenience that may grow

thereby is seen in many histories both ancient and modern. But when you see the naked blade or weapon, consider that it means redress of wrong, justice and revenge. Therefore if he be your friend that will needs fight with you, you may tell him that you have given him no cause, nor offered any wrong, and if any other have made any false report, that his is to prove and justify it, that for yourself, if by chance without your knowledge you have offended him, that you are ready with reason to satisfy him and make amends. But if they be matters that touch your honor and that you be compelled to accept of the combat, do the best you can when you have your weapon in your hand, and consider that fights are dangerous, and you know not the mind and purpose of your enemy, whom if you should chance to spare, afterwards peradventure he may kill you or put you in danger of your life, especially when you use the mandritta or right blows: for if he be either a man skillful at his weapon, or fiery or furious, he may peradventure do that to you, which you would not do, (when you might) to him. Wherefore if he be your friend go not with him into the field, but if you go, do your best, because it seems childish to say, I will go and fight, but I will spare and favor him. (Jackson 217–18)

His advice is still sound. Don't fight with friends. In any fight, not knowing your opponent's intentions, the prudent course is to presume he means you harm, since even if he means you none, he may wound or kill you by accident. If you succeed in just wounding someone, forcing him to surrender, now as in Saviolo's time, it's unlikely he will thank you for his mutilation, and he may come back later (perhaps not alone) for revenge.

Single Rapier (Espada Sola)

Saviolo begins his scholar's instruction with the single rapier, seeing it as the ground (the musical metaphor was not lost on his pupils) of all his technique. He argues whether the rapier technique "is not much more rare and excellent than any other, considering that a man, having the perfect knowledge and practice of this art, although of small stature and weaker strength, may, with a little removing of his foot, a sudden turning of his hand, a slight declin-

ing of his body, subdue and overcome the fierce braving pride of
tall and strong bodies" (Jackson 192).

After explaining the principles of footwork, offense, and defense
Saviolo suggests that rapier techniques can be applied to all other
weapons, including rapier and dagger. Saviolo also notes that the
single rapier should be mastered first because it was then the
weapon of choice for most gentlemen. Saviolo's position is that
rapier fundamentals learned step-by-step provide an inestimable
basis for all martial skills. Without such teachings a person had no
chance of learning the secret tricks, or the advanced techniques,
that added to the mystique of the fencing master.

Stance and Grip

Saviolo teaches one basic stance for both salon and field. He uses
it for both single rapier and rapier-dagger, claiming that the stance
is used in the wars (especially in single rapier) by Italians, French,
Spanish, and Germans, all countries where the art was highly
developed. This was a practice deplored by the military strategist
Smythe (43). Saviolo also maintains that his stance forces in-
fighting, making your opponent come to you.

Saviolo's basic stance begins with the right foot forward, knees
bent, with the weight resting somewhat more on the left leg (see
Figure 6). As Saviolo puts it, so "that his body rest more upon the
left leg, not steadfast and firm as some stand, which seem to be
nailed to the place, but with a readiness and nimbleness" (Jackson
212). (As Hamlet tells Horatio just before his fencing match "the
readiness is all" [V, 2, 211].)

The rapier is brought short, that is with the arm bent, the hilt
just outside the right knee, the point threatening the opponent's
face (see Figure 7). This is very similar to Di Grassi's low ward.
Saviolo gives sound strategic reasons for keeping the rapier pulled
in close to the body, instead of extended straight out, as in the
Spanish style.[5] It has been suggested that Saviolo advocated (and
many illustrations of the time show this) holding the rapier low
because it was too heavy to hold upright for prolonged periods.
Practical experience with replica rapiers has taught us that it can be
exhausting, but the Spanish, among others, thought the defensive
advantages outweighed the fatigue and loss of speed. But for

Figure 6. Saviolo's basic stance. (By permission of the Folger Shakespeare Library)

Figure 7. This illustration from Saviolo is of the basic stance, but now the rapiers are engaged, with both fighters taking the outside line to the opponent. This is also called crossing swords. (By permission of the Folger Shakespeare Library)

Saviolo's style of quick and nimble play, he suggests "let him make his hand free and at liberty, not by force of the arm, but by the nimble and ready moving of the joint of the wrist of the hand, so that his hand be free and at liberty from his body," and therefore ready for the deadly counterstrike (see Figure 8) (Jackson 212).

Figure 8. An illustration from Saviolo showing two fighters in basic stance, but the one on the right has initiated a shift onto the front foot prior to an attack. Note the use of the relaxed unarmed hands as protection. (By permission of the Folger Shakespeare Library)

Saviolo's style was thought restrained in as much as he taught that when a person's weapon is drawn, he should put himself in his safest guard and wait for the opponent to make the first move, all the while seeking the advantage. There must have been many, many fighters—demonstrating typical swordplay from some other Italian school, or simply through natural aggressiveness—who threw themselves into the attack, hoping by a furious assault to overwhelm the opponent. Di Grassi, Saviolo, and Silver all agree on this point and cite numerous lamentable examples of stout gentlemen slain (often simultaneously) in rushing each other. Saviolo stresses again and again, "put yourself well in guard, seeking the advantage of your enemy, and leap not up and down" (Jackson 259).

The debate is ages old over who has the advantage (presuming fighters of equal skill): the fighter who strikes first (the thruster), or the fighter who counters the first attack and launches a lightning counterstrike (to the Elizabethans, the warder). There is a famous scene in Kurosawa's *Seven Samurai* that illustrates this principle beautifully. A wise old samurai and his protégé are scouring the town for samurai to join them. They notice a crowd gathering at the wall of a vacant lot, breathlessly watching two samurai preparing a duel with fresh-cut sword-lengths of bamboo. The older, slightly built duelist slowly comes on guard. His rough-looking opponent quickly comes on guard in opposition, making several quick weight shifts, foot movements, and feints accompanied by fierce shouts. The wise old samurai and his protégé look from one fencer to the other in the long moment before the first blow. The rough duelist charges, trying to gain the advantage with speed and surprise. The older duelist waits and makes no attempt to avoid the oncoming attack; instead he delivers a devastating counterattack a split second before being hit himself. The rough duelist claims it a tie and the older duelist disagrees, claiming "a real sword would kill you." The rough fencer shouts in rage and real swords are drawn. "How stupid," says the wise old samurai, "it's so obvious." The scene is replayed, this time for life and death, and the older duelist wins, just as he predicted.

Saviolo teaches the modern notion of *en guarde* at least a hundred years before that idea was formalized.[6] To be en guarde means holding the body in such a way that the greatest possible number of lines of attack are well defended, forcing your opponent either to attack you where you've deliberately left yourself open, or force you to close the opening you've left and open another. A fighter in this posture is said to be engaged, and some means must be found to force an opening in his defense (dis-engaging). Albert Manley describes the modern fencing guard as a guard/invitation, since when one guards against a certain attack, he opens himself to an attack somewhere else—in fact, he expects/invites it. In addition, Manley explains, "the well known command, 'on guard,' merely means 'Be alert' or 'Look out!' It is not the position that saves you, but your vigilance and ability to move" (51).

Saviolo prefigures this modern strategy, listing detailed and extensive advantages for this short guard. For example:

You must especially take heed that you put not your self in
danger, because if your enemy should find you without your
sword at length, being nimble and strong, striking upon your
weapon he might make a passage with great speed and make
himself master as well of you as of your weapon, and put you
in danger of your life. Whereas contrary-wise, when you do
hold your rapier short, as I have told you, and that your point
is towards his face, you make him afraid, especially when he
comes forward with his hand and body to find your weapon
with his, he must needs come so far that you may easily hurt
him without being hurt. Besides all this if your enemy should
deliver a stoccata , imbroccata, mandritta, or riversa, you have
great advantage, for he cannot so readily strike, nor with such
surety as you may. (Jackson 237)

To grip the rapier, Saviolo reasonably advises that each scholar
take what's "commodious," but cautions against the grip with two
fingers over the hilt. Instead he advocates the thumb on the hilt
and only one finger over the *quillons*.[7] According to him (and our
practical experience with museum-grade replicas bears him out),
when thrusting with two fingers locked over the *quillons*, the point
has a more pronounced tendency to stray upward from the straight
line to impact, especially with a tight grip. Hooking the second
finger over the *quillons* also makes it more difficult to observe his
injunction: "let him make his hand free and at liberty, not by force
of the arm, but by the nimble and ready moving of the joint of
the wrist . . . so that his hand be free and at liberty from his body
and that the ward of his hand be directly against his right knee"
(Jackson 212).

Distance and Footwork

The teacher and student come on guard very close to one another.
Their rapiers cross in the middle, their front feet right against one
another. Though Saviolo forces Luke to fight at the minimal limit
of effective close fighting distance—evidently a training technique
for demonstration purposes—as a general rule he advocates laying
farther off.

His "just" distance is defined as close enough to hit your opponent with only a small step forward. He points out the fencer's

age-old dilemma: if you are close enough to hit your opponent, he is close enough to hit you. Therefore the old maxim says that fencing is the art of "touching without being touched." Then as now, the answer to this dilemma lies in the perception of this "just" distance. If you can perceive this distance and your opponent cannot, or if you can perceive it before your opponent, you gain a distinct momentary advantage. The strategic wisdom is, never come within distance until you choose, and conversely, never let your opponent into distance, for as Saviolo says:

> and note this well, that to seek to offend, being out of measure, and not in due time, is very dangerous: . . . having put yourself in guard . . . take heed how you go about, and that your right foot be foremost, stealing the advantage by little and little, carrying your left leg behind, with your point within the point of your enemy's sword, and so finding the advantage in time and measure, make a stoccata to the belly [a thrust from a low position, under the opponent's weapon] or face of your enemy, as you shall find him unguarded. (Jackson 231)

This "stealing" step, some 100 years before it is acknowledged to have been invented, is the same now used in modern fencing. Saviolo did not recommend it for basic footwork however, believing that attacking in a straight line was a grievous strategic error. The preferred course was to slip to the right or left, as modern boxers do, attempting to gain the advantage. For initiating offense as well, Saviolo maintains that the straight line is not good and the circular attack is better for controlling the opponent's weapon. Despite its obvious defensive advantages, it was thought a disgrace by most English to give ground or back up before an advancing opponent. But the wily Saviolo notes, "There is a difference between retiring orderly and running backward, for to hit and retire is not discommendable. . . . [We] see the like in martial policy, where oftentimes retreats are made of purpose to draw the enemy either into some ambush or place of advantage" (Jackson 254–55).

Saviolo agrees with the Spaniards in advocating side-stepping avoidances. The hallmark of the Spanish rapier school was a mystic belief in the advantage to be gained by moving to the side along the radius of an imaginary circle defined by the combatants. Their system, called the *Destrezza,* was based partly on Euclid's geometry and partly on the movements of animals, such as dogs or fighting cocks, that circle each other in combat.[8] Silver claimed that "The Spaniard is now thought to be a better man with his rapier than is the Italian, Frenchmen, High Almaine [German] or any other countryman whatsoever" (Jackson 511). Ben Jonson's most famous fencing references are of the Spanish school. However, without resorting to geometrical or mystical references, Saviolo advocates the side-step "circle-wise" in almost every case. This circle-wise step is Di Grassi's compass (see chapter 2).

Apparently this removing to the side, which sometimes involved crossing the line of attack, was not common. Luke protests: "This play which now you tell me of, methinks is contrary to many other, and I myself have seen many play and teach clean after another fashion, for I have seen them all remove in a right line [like modern fencing] . . . which . . . is best to use, either the right or the circular line?" Saviolo replies: "When you stand upon this ward, if you remove in a straight line . . . your adversary may give you a stoccata either in the belly or in the face. Besides, if your adversary have a dagger he may do the like, hitting you with his dagger either in the belly or in the face, besides other harms which I list not to write . . . it is not good" (Jackson 222).

Offensive Strategy

Like Di Grassi, Saviolo extols the thrust over the cut in no uncertain terms, "for to tell the truth, I would not advise any friend of mine, if he were to fight for his credit and his life, to strike neither mandrittas nor riversas [types of cuts, explained below], because he puts himself in danger of his life. To use the point is more ready, and spends not the like time" (Jackson 211). Though the modern lunge is said not to have been invented until Capo Ferro in 1610, Saviolo detailed movements that fulfill almost all the definitions of a lunge, viz., delivery of the thrust by carrying the right foot forward, followed by a retiring of the right foot (Castle 163).[9] Saviolo advised, "you may thrust your stoccata either at his face or breast, but do it with great promptness, and in the same time recoil with your left foot drawing after your right, and be quick in the retire to recover your rapier, that if your enemy make forward, you may be ready again to thrust" (Jackson 294). The only difference between his description and the modern lunge, as far as the lower body is concerned, is that in modern fencing the left foot remains stationary throughout.

Thrusts

Saviolo speaks throughout primarily of three types of thrusts. The imbroccata is executed with the hand in pronation (knuckles forward, i.e., the palm faces outward, to the right) over the opponent's sword or dagger hand and downward; he also sometimes calls it a *foin*.[10] The stoccata is the reverse of the imbroccata, reaching the opponent under his sword or dagger with the hand in supination (knuckles downward, nails upward), also called the thrust. The punta riversa, made famous by Shakespeare, is delivered from the left side (Di Grassi's inside line), usually on a step, with the hand in supination, and may be directed either over or under the opponent's weapon hand.[11] Ultimately, Saviolo maintains "all the skill of this art in effect is nothing but a stoccata" (Jackson 239).

When thrusting, Saviolo's preferred targets are the belly, and most especially the face. Almost all his simultaneous counterattacks (stop-hits) are to the face.[12] The debilitating effects of even a grazing hit in the face or head can be readily appreciated, as cuts on the face or scalp bleed profusely. Puncture wounds anywhere on the head easily can be fatal. Short of an outright kill, Saviolo notes "Every little hit in the face stayeth the fury of a man more than any other place in his body" (Aylward, *The English Master of Arms* 58). He also notes that blood in the eyes will dissuade most opponents, and many a man choked on his own blood when breathing heavily. Saviolo particularly advocates it since most Englishmen were used to the school practice (known as scholar's privilege) of avoiding the face completely. This can be a deadly habit, leading to two mistakes: either not taking sufficient defensive precautions against your opponent's thrusts to your face, or failing to use his weakness (in doing the same) against him. As a result of this error, English fencing masters were notorious for having only one eye. Sir Thomas Overbury claimed that a Master who had more than one eye was a lucky man (Aylward, *The English Master of Arms* 36).[13]

Cuts

Saviolo's discussion of cuts incorporates Di Grassi's descriptions (see chapter 2). He demonstrates cuts in the first lessons primarily in playing the typical English fight. Three types of cuts are discussed, all for offensive use, in order to learn the proper defense against the English reliance on them. Throughout the first lesson, Saviolo role-plays the typical English fight, responding to the scholar's thrust usually with a left-hand parry and a sidestep, followed by a cut.

The mandritta is a horizontal cut, with the palm up, from right to left, delivered with the right edge of the blade (the knuckle edge as opposed to the false or back edge), and consequently landing on the opponent's left side. The riversi is, as it's name suggests, the reverse of the mandritta. The riversi is usually delivered horizontally from the left to the right, palm down, with the right edge (sometimes called the true edge) landing on the opponent's right side.[14] And finally, there is the stramazone, similar to the moulinet used in today's sabre fence. The stramazone is a quick vertical cut to the head, palm to the left, with the right edge. It is defined by Stone as "a tearing cut with the extreme point" (584). Saviolo warns: "and if he offer you a stramazone to the head, you must bear it with your sword; passing forward with your left leg and turning well your hand, that your point may go in the nature of an imbroccata, accompanied with your left hand so that your point always respects the belly of your adversary. And break this always with the point of your sword, for of all stoccatas, riversas and stramazones, I find it the most dangerous" (Jackson 232).

Luke protests that everyone (meaning especially every "down-right" Englishman) knew how to cut with his sword. But as Saviolo explains, there is a fundamental difference between the hacking cut with the English sword and the slicing cut with a rapier. The mistake most often made was getting in too close to give a proper drawing or slicing cut with the rapier. This may have been simply because most Englishmen were used to the (often) shorter English sword, and therefore routinely misjudged the correct distance with rapier.

V. Yes, every man can strike, but every man has not the skill to strike, especially with measure, and to make it cut. And hereupon you shall see many which oftentimes will strike and hit with the flat of their rapier, without hurting or wounding the adversary. And likewise many, when they would strike a downright blow, will go forward more than measure, and so cause themselves to be slain. Wherefore I say, when the master and scholar shall stand upon this ward, and that the point of the scholar's weapon shall be against the face of the teacher, and the point of the teacher's weapon nigh to the ward of the scholar's rapier, and that it be stretched out then the scholar shall remove with his right foot a little aside in circle wise, and with the inside of his left hand barrachet-wise shall beat away his master's rapier, first lifting his above it, and let the left foot follow the right: and let him turn skillfully his body, or else he shall be in danger to receive a stoccata either in the face or belly. Therefore he must take heed to save himself with good time and measure, and let him take heed that he step not forward toward his teacher, for so he should be in danger to be wounded: but let him go a little aside as I have already said. (Jackson 216)

He also gives the method of cutting that eliminates the possibility of striking with the flat instead of the edge of the blade. He points out that the scholar must lead with his knuckles (turn his knuckles) toward the target of the cut to avoid hitting with the flat.

Defense

For Saviolo there was no real parry with the rapier. Instead, the most salient feature of the Italian defensive fight was reliance on the *time*. The time is now generally known as the time-thrust, or stop-hit. Docciolini defined it in 1601: "when thine enemy thrusts at thee, break thou his thrust, striking him at the same time" (Castle 139). In general, parries against thrusts are executed with the left hand. Against cuts, the sword opposes in a simultaneous counterattack, almost always a thrust.

In other words, the ultimate strategy is to avoid the attack, and simultaneously reattack. Saviolo plays on the reluctance of fighters to be hit in the face (Englishmen in particular seemed to find it unsporting or dishonorable). This became something of a secret move of his school, a hallmark.

Whilst your enemy strikes his mandritta, you deliver a strong
thrust or stoccata to his face. For the avoiding of which, he
must need shrink back, otherwise he is slain: and how little
soever your enemy is wounded in the face, he is half undone
and vanquished, whether by chance it fall out that the blood
cover and hinder his sight, or that the wound be mortal, as
most in that part are. And it is an easy matter to one which
knows this play, to hit the face, although everyone understands
not this advantage. And many there are which have practiced
and do practice fence, and which have to deal with those
which understand these kinds of thrusts or stoccatas, and yet
cannot learn to use them, unless the secrets be shown them.
Because these matters are for fight and combat, not for play
or practice. (Jackson 232)

As Saviolo points out, hitting in the face wasn't allowed in class
for obvious reasons, so few school-trained fighters gave it proper
offensive or (especially) defensive attention. Also, the face cannot
be protected as the belly can (his other prime target) with a
concealed coat of mail as was the practice in his native Italy.[15]

He goes as far as to advise never to parry thrusts with the rapier
(of course, every rule has its exceptions). Quite prudently, he advises
wearing a leather or mail glove on the left hand, telling us that the
rapier and glove are "most in use among gentlemen." Some scholars
claim this is what Shakespeare intended for the fencing bout in
Hamlet for example.[16] For, as Saviolo says, "it were better to hazard
a little hurt of the hand, thereby to become master of his enemy's
sword, than to [parry] with the sword, and so give the enemy the
advantage . . . moreover, having the use of your left hand, and wearing a gauntlet or glove of mail, your enemy shall no sooner make a
thrust, but you shall be ready to catch his sword fast, and so command him at your pleasure: wherefore I wish you not to defend any
thrust with the sword" (Jackson 228).

In addition to breaking the opponent's thrust, he places great
emphasis on escaping the thrusts by passing, voiding, "playing with
your bodies, removing with your feet a little aside, winding of your
bodies" as Silver scornfully noted (Morsberger 25). Usually these
defensive avoidances were to the side, "circle-wise." For example,
"At the same time the scholar removes his foot, the teacher shall play

a little with stirring of his body, and with his left hand shall beat away his scholar's Rapier from his right side, and shall remove his right foot behind his left striking a cross blow at the head" (Jackson 213).

This voiding to the side is a hallmark of the Italian style. The Spanish also advocated going to the side along an imaginary circle, but they held their bodies upright and apparently made their traverses rather slowly. Saviolo continually saves himself in encounters Luke is sure would be fatal, by shifting a little with his body. Naturally this movement is an advanced skill. The student is advised not to rely on it. It is acquired only after many hours of practice and is akin to the "ball-sense" of a professional athlete, i.e., the ability to anticipate the trajectory of an incoming rapier's point from certain clues in the movements of the opponent. It is a prerogative of the master in the lessons, like using a lighter rapier or a shirt of mail.[17]

The ultimate defensive strategy, as in modern Kendo, was to put oneself on guard and to wait for the opening provided when the opponent began his attack, and to time him. Saviolo endorses the warder, he who goes not leaping but stands firm and ready for the sudden deadly counterattacking movement. As he says, "Either of you being within distance observing time, the first offerer is in danger to be slain or wounded in the counter-time especially if he thrust resolutely; but if you be skillful, and not the other, then you may gain time and measure and so hit him, saving yourself" (Jackson 253). He disdains the peculiarly English notion that your opponent should be allowed "first shot." "Some of the opinion that they can hit him that shall hit them first, but such have never fought; or if by chance in one fight they have been so fortunate, let them not think that summer is come because one swallow is seen" (Jackson 254). As with the medieval Japanese samurai, the result of two skilled swordsmen simultaneously applying this strategy was a tense standoff.

Specialty Moves (*Botte Secrete*)
Seizure-Disarms

Saviolo then moves to explaining simultaneous attack and seizure of the opponent's blade, pointing out that when performed with quick agility it is an excellent technique. The optimum position for an attempted seizure of your opponent's blade occurs when he holds his point at length, not toward your face. The scholar then must simultaneously beat aside his opponent's rapier with his left hand, not at the point, but toward the middle, and move in with his left foot against the right foot of the opponent. The scholar then opposes the master's blade with his and seizes the rapier-guard, not the hand. As he points out, if you grab the hand and not the weapon, an experienced opponent will grab the point of his weapon with his left hand, leveraging it into you. A seizure of this sort may be well what is indicated in the stage direction in *Hamlet* (V, ii): "In scuffling, they change rapiers."

Inquartata

The inquartata is often confused with the lunge. It is used as a stop-hit, and it involves a side step with the rear foot (or sometimes just a long step back) away from opponent's thrust, together with a lowering of the body underneath the incoming blade. The left hand usually rests on the ground for balance, and when one has evaded the thrust by ducking under it, the arm is straightened, letting the opponent "run on" it. This was also known as the *passata sotto* and may be Mercutio's referent, "Come sir, your passado," in *Romeo and Juliet* (III, i, 83). Saviolo also speaks of the half-inquartata. The move in modern fencing is sometimes called the three-point lunge.

Rapier and Dagger

The second part of Saviolo's first book is divided into four "day's discourses." Three concern the rapier and dagger, the last the single rapier for the left-handed.

Saviolo says, "as far as I can perceive the rules of the single rapier, and of the rapier and dagger are all one" (Jackson 252). The thrusts and cuts, tactical considerations, and footwork remain the same. Instead of thrusts being parried with the left hand, they are now parried with the dagger.

Like the single rapier, all rapier and dagger techniques should be executed at one time. The stop-hit, for example, is as effective with rapier and dagger as with single rapier. Saviolo diverges sharply with Silver on this point for both rapier and rapier-dagger.

For example, Silver maintained that the foot should precede the hand in delivering thrusts.

The most salient divergence from single rapier play, of course, is that now the left hand plays an offensive role as well. Silver claimed that against stabs from daggers at close range there was no defense. For example, Steinmetz gives the following gruesome description of a 1609 rapier and dagger encounter: "They attacked each other, each armed with a rapier and a dagger. In the first onset, Cheek ran Dutton through the throat with his dagger, close to the windpipe; then Dutton made a pass at him and ran him through the body, while he stabbed [Cheek] in the back with his poniard" (173).

Stance and Footwork

The basic stance for rapier and dagger is the same as that advocated for single rapier. The scholar puts his right foot forward, with weight somewhat on the left leg, both knees slightly bent. The rapier is held short, that is, with the hilt just outside the right knee. The point of the rapier menaces the opponent's face, and the dagger is held out straight, at arm's length, with the point also menacing the opponent's face (see figures 9 and 10). Luke points out that more usually he has seen the dagger pointing upward, as in defending a riversa (see Silver's illustration, Figure 11, in chapter 4). But, as practical experience on the authors' part has shown, parrying a strong cut with the dagger alone is a rare skill purchased with many bruises and bashed knuckles on the training room floor. Saviolo advises correctly that he who holds the point upwards is ever in danger to be hit in the face, hand, or belly.

He describes in the "second day's discourse" the punta riversa ward or stance, noting that it is in many ways the opposite or contrary stance and especially hard to learn. This stance is similar to the one above, with the rapier short, but within the right knee, on the left side. The dagger is still carried with arm outstretched, dagger threatening the opponent's face. The punta riversa can then be executed with a "pass with your right foot towards the right side of your enemy, so that your right foot be somewhat on the outside of your enemy's right foot" (Jackson 275).

In detailing various attack combinations, Saviolo notes other

Figure 9. An illustration from Saviolo showing two fighters with rapier and dagger. Note that both fighters have stepped (circular step) back with the right foot, thus keeping the defensive dagger well in front. (By permission of the Folger Shakespeare Library)

Figure 10. An illustration from Saviolo of a variation with rapier and dagger. The points of both dagger and rapier are forward, and the legs are in basic stance. Compare to Figure 8. (By permission of the Folger Shakespeare Library)

(inferior) stances, including: with rapier long and straight, dagger aloft; rapier short with dagger pointed up (an open ward, see Silver illustration, Figure 11); with rapier aloft, pointing downward and dagger at the knee (a particularly spectacular but foolhardy guard, Saviolo gives four effective attack combinations against it); and a final popular guard with rapier and dagger outstretched upon each other, crosswise.

Offense

Attacks with rapier and dagger are consistent with single rapier, relying on the thrust rather than the cut. The dagger is used primarily for defense not offense, except as noted above, when the fighters are close together. The situation then is equally deadly to both, with indiscriminate stabbing and very little chance of defense. Instead, Saviolo uses the rapier for all stoccatas, imbroccatas, and so forth. The dagger is used offensively only to move the opponent's blade aside for a thrust with the rapier. In executing any move taking the enemy's rapier, with dagger either under or over, he stresses that you keep the arm straight and firm, because of the danger of running on the enemy's weapon.

Defense

Thrusts are usually parried with the dagger to the outside (left). The only exception is against an imbroccata by a riversa which may be broken to the inside, but must be accompanied by a slight retreat of the body and replied with a swift riversa. Saviolo advocates the double parry, with both rapier and dagger, at least twice as often as does Di Grassi, particularly against high cuts.

In defending with the dagger, he repeatedly enjoins the scholar to "hold your dagger firm, marking as it were with one eye the motion of your adversary, and with the other the advantage of thrusting" (Jackson 263). It is particularly deadly to move the entire arm when parrying with the dagger, because of the danger of the opponent "falsifying" and redirecting his attack over or under the displaced dagger. Therefore Saviolo advises keeping the arm straight, and bending only the wrist to point the dagger up or down, as the attack dictates.

As with single rapier, the best defense is the "time." This may be executed by opposing the attack with either rapier or dagger, or with both, and simultaneously turning the hand and voiding the body in such a way that the opponent cannot help but be hit. Alternatively, as before, Saviolo is a great proponent of the quick thrust, particularly to the face, on the inception of the opponent's offensive move. Perhaps the archetypical Saviolo "time," requiring agility, readiness, and resolution, is the quick stoccata to the face as the opponent draws back for a good edge blow.

Having already detailed the punta riversa offensively, Saviolo explains the defense against it. "If your enemy make towards your right side and offer a thrust, happily pressing too much forward, you shall immediately turn your body on the left side, so that the point of his rapier passing beside your body, you may give him a stoccata: or you may play with your body and beat his rapier point outward from your right side with your dagger and give him a punta riversa over his rapier in the belly or face" (Jackson 276).

The final "day's discourse" indicates how a left-handed fighter handles one that is righthanded. The common lore of the day was that a southpaw had some advantage in a fight. Probably it was true that if there were few left-handed fencers, they may have dismayed some fencers who lacked a system and relied only on select moves taught to them. Luke claims that left-handers have a great advantage. Saviolo notes that this is a commonly and strongly held belief, but he wisely replies, "the left hand has no advantage of the right, nor the right of the left . . . only use and knowledge gives the better to either" (Jackson 303). Saviolo deflates the power of this superstition by enjoining his scholar simply to remember when facing a left-hander, that he'll do everything opposite the way it looks with a right-hander. The fencer must stay cool and not be thrown by the difference in look. A thrust is a thrust, whether from a right hand or left.

Conclusion

Finally, Luke asks what stance Saviolo would teach to him who finds himself in desperate need of his first instruction, shortly before a duel. Saviolo recommends a guard easily learned and maximally effective, with the left foot forward and both rapier and dagger outstretched as far as possible. For defense from this guard (against an opponent in the standard right-forward stance), he advocates a traverse towards the opponent's left side, thrusting a quick stoccata to the face. Saviolo points out that this guard is particularly well suited to commanding the enemy's rapier with your dagger in preparation for a thrust, especially if the enemy ignores Saviolo's advice and holds his rapier long and not short.

To defend against an opponent in this "one only ward," Saviolo says that in charging him on either the left or right side, if he passes on his right foot, "do but change your body to your left side, lifting up the point of your poniard, firming your hand on your right knee. So shall you be master of his sword, and may easily strike him. And the more fierce he is, the more shall you command his weapon and endanger him" (Jackson 292). In conclusion, he reiterates that his first guard (right foot forward, rapier short, and dagger held outright) is the best against the above guard or any other, though it takes more practice.

Of course, no amount of diligent study in the salon guarantees success in a duel. Luke notes that "although a man learn perfectly the [man]dritta, riversa, the stoccata, the imbroccata, the punta riversa, with each several motion of the body, yet when they come to single fight . . . they utterly forget all their former practices" (Jackson 285). Saviolo's answer is diligent practice, maintaining that it will help the furious man to retain his reason, give courage to those who are nervous, and even help him who may have had too much to drink.

PARADOXES

OF DEFENCE,

WHEREIN IS PROVED THE TRVE
grounds of Fight to be in the short auncient weapons,
and that the short Sword hath aduantage of the long
Sword or long Rapier. And the weakenesse and imperfection of the Rapier-fights displayed, Together with an
Admonition to the noble, ancient, victorious, valiant,
and most braue nation of Englishmen, to beware of false
teachers of Defence, and how they forsake their owne
naturall fights : with a briefe commendation of
the noble science or exercising of
Armes.

By George Siluer Gentleman.

LONDON,
Printed for Edvvard Blount.
1599.

AN ADMONITION
TO THE NOBLE, ANCIENT,
VICTORIOVS, VALIANT, AND
MOST BRAVE NATION OF
ENGLISHMEN.

Eorge Siluer hauing the perfect knowledge of all maner of weapõs, and being experiẽced in all maner of fights, thereby perceiuing the great abuses by the *Italian* Teachers of Offence done vnto them, the great errors, inconueniences, & false resolutions they haue brought them into, haue inforced me, euen of pitie of their most lamentable wounds and slaughters, & as I verily thinke it my bounden dutie, with all loue and humilitie to admonish them to take heed, how they submit themselues into the hands of *Italian* teachers of Defence, or straungers whatsoeuer; and to beware how they forsake or suspect their owne naturall fight, that they may by casting off of these Italianated, weake, fantasticall, and most diuellish and imperfect fights, and by exercising of their owne ancient weapons, be restored, or atchieue vnto their natural, and most manly and victorious fight againe, the dint and force whereof manie

B

4

The English Reply:
George Silver and His
Paradoxes of Defence

By 1599, the rapier and dagger had become the most talked-about new weapons in England. Most swordsmen were rapidly acquainting themselves with the new techniques, though we should not forget that for the lower classes, a rapier-dagger fight was usually seen only from afar. Due to increased quantities and lower costs, the English sword (supplemented by the usual sticks, knives, cudgels, and bare hands) was much more likely to be found as part of general brawls. In any case, for the upper-class gentleman, the rapier offered a unique combination of "skill, deftness and courage" that seemed to symbolize traditional qualities of the courtly tradition (Brailsford 29).

True-blue English fencing masters, however, still had not entirely capitulated to the new style. We have only bits and pieces of correspondence and descriptions of actual events in what must have been an intriguing battle of propaganda between the old and new style teachers. George Silver's work, *Paradoxes of Defence,* is such an example—the only surviving fencing manual from the sixteenth century written by an Englishman—of the lengths to which the English masters were forced to go to retain their influence.

Many of Silver's ideas and techniques have value. They should not automatically be dismissed as worthless. Particularly in his insistence on real combat conditions, Silver injects a note of somber reality to the whole subject of swordplay. Other critics (Wise, Castle) have often given Silver only brief consideration, due not only to his investment in a losing style, but also to his off-putting sarcasm and tone. Silver frequently overstates his case against the rapier.

Despite this, behind his invective there are grains of truth, as we shall see. Although Silver was running counter to the flow of events and was eventually left behind by the new swordplay techniques, it is his commitment to the traditional ways that leaves us with an excellent example of the English style prior to the rapier's arrival. As an historical document, in addition to its rather brief description of techniques, the *Paradoxes* represents the last gasp of a dying breed: the conservative—even reactionary—voice of a man watching his beloved Englishman's style receding before waves of enthusiasm for the Italian rapier.

George Silver prefers to describe himself as a gentleman, albeit one who has "perfect knowledge of all manner of weapons" (Jackson 499). He was a descendant of Sir Bartholomew Silver who had been knighted by Edward II. Married to Mary Haydon on March 24, 1579 or 1580, he was also granted letters of patent with his partner, Sir Arthur Aston, on August 22, 1604, to finance an experiment in logwood. Such a gilded past suggests that he "never dreamed of being taken for a mere professional teacher of the sword," and hints at why he only refers to the English Masters of Defense as though from afar, though not without cordial respect (Aylward, *The English Master of Arms* 63). No more of his personal history is known.

Invoking the notion of everlasting truth in his "Dedicatorie" (to Robert Earl of Essex, Saviolo's patron), Silver appraises the sad state of fencing. His countrymen are too often led to "chop and change, turn and return, from ward to ward, from fight to fight, in this unconstant search, yet we never rest in any, and that because we never find the truth" (Jackson 493). For Silver, the cult of the rapier is only the latest of such mistaken attempts to replace the older standards of weaponry with newfangled systems.

He then suggests that the true weapon for an Englishman must be the short sword and such weapons of "perfect length," rather than in "long Swords, long Rapiers, [and] frog pricking Poiniards [daggers]" (Jackson 493). Teaching a system based on false or impractical weapons such as these only confuses students and provokes dangerous hesitations in fighting. "To prove this, I have set forth these my Paradoxes, different I confess from the main current of our outlandish teachers, but agreeing I am well assured to the truth, and tending as I hope to the honor of our English nation" (Jackson 494).

But Silver cannot resist continuing his diatribe just a while longer: "we, like degenerate sons, have forsaken our forefather's virtues with their weapons and have lusted like men sick of a strange ague, after the strange vices and devices of Italian, French and Spanish Fencers, little remembering, that these Apish toys could not free Rome from Brennius' sack, nor France from King Henry the Fifth his conquest" (Jackson 494). His reference to Brennius is not only a classical allusion; it may also hint at the Italian teachers' common contention that the Romans invented the thrust. Henry V is a bit of deliberate flag-waving.

Silver summons the memories of Ajax and Achilles as true models for English swordplay, comparing the new rapier stylists to pygmies who fight with bodkins. In his most serious indictment, however, he charges that rapier play has encouraged lawless fighting in peace time, and yet such "bird spits" are not fit for use in battle (Jackson 496).

Although the changing nature of warfare at the end of the sixteenth century—with the widespread use of gunpowder, cavalry, and archers—made such an accusation mostly irrelevant, it highlights the widening differences between personal combat and battle.[1] Traditionally, when called to fight for his country, the average Englishman searched through trunks and cupboards to find his trusty sword and shield before leaving his family. This is the weapon Silver refers to.

In contrast, the rapier was more a part of daily dressing for around-town wear. The rapier was not a pedigreed weapon of warfare; it was invented and modified by various fencing masters in the rarified atmosphere of late sixteenth century court society. The quickening popularity of dueling throughout Europe only accelerated rapier play as a unique, class-bound way of settling private scores. As its use widened to include the French, Spanish, German—and eventually the English—upper classes, it retained this snob appeal.

If made a hundred years before, Silver's charge that the rapier was useless in battle would have been a powerful argument. As it is, such a statement only points up how out of step his thinking was in this matter. Elizabethan military theorists and practitioners had already long left behind discussions regarding edged weapons.

Of more concern to military theorists such as Smythe were the uses of the bow and the lance (which were also rapidly being supplanted by gunpowder). Nonetheless, Silver's introduction gives us fair warning that he is not about to offer more of the latest fashion in swordplay.

In being out of touch with the latest cultural currents, however, *Paradoxes of Defence* is as much an example of Elizabethan social/cultural thought as it is of fight technique. Italian notions of honor—ideas brought from the Italian court society to the English and allowed to trickle down through the upper class—were sown through the writings of such authors as Castiglione and Sir Thomas Elyot, among others. Although the political situations between the European nations and England were in almost constant turmoil during this period, there was still enormous curiosity regarding new discoveries in foreign lands. In addition, the growing need on the part of the English upper classes to find lifestyles peculiar to them alone was revising the notions of what a true gentleman might be and of what things honor consisted. Silver gives the impression of stubbornly resisting all such influences and contemporary events. He is more exemplary of a kind of English middle-class insularity that "arises out of a sense of national insecurity when faced with outside innovation" (Arthur Wise, *The Art and History of Personal Combat* 57).[2]

As another aspect of that middle-classness, we must not overlook a more deep-seated reason for Silver's attack on the rapier: rapier swordplay was not only too dangerous, it was too refined. There is a long tradition in England of a love of fighting for its own sake, and rough and tumble bouts with blunted weapons, as well as wrestling and boxing, were popular diversions in Elizabethan England.

In contrast, rapiers required even more coolness and discipline. Perhaps part of Silver's objection to the new weapon lay in its studied seriousness. A thrust, even with a blunted weapon, presented a much greater danger to the fencer than did a blow. The old sense of horseplay and high spirits that characterized such typical English amusements as cudgel fights and bareknuckle bouts was gone in rapier swordplay.

Although we will explore what Silver's technical and theoretical objections to rapier play were—and some of those objections had merit—a reactionary attitude drives much of his writing. This makes the *Paradoxes* more than a manual of technical fencing skills: it provides a window to a significant aspect of Elizabethan cultural history. Silver's personal biases—probably common to many Englishmen who remained unconvinced of the rapier's worth—must be kept in mind when analyzing all levels of his argument.

The Dangers of Italian Swordplay

The author begins the body of his text with a plea (using Italian or Italianate with obvious distaste four times in the first eighteen lines) to all brave Englishmen, to "cast off these Italianated, weak, fantastical, and most devilish and imperfect fights, and by exercising their own ancient weapons, be restored . . . their natural, and most manly and victorious fight again" (Jackson 499). Silver's quarrel is not with weapon training per se, far from it. He respects the Masters of Defense, by which he means the English Masters. He also lists a variety of physical skills and character-building attributes that may be developed by the physical and mental study of swordplay.

But he says it is traditional English swordplay that is needed, preferably taught by a good Englishman. In a bit of self-serving chauvinism, Silver proclaims it is only because the English are so friendly to foreigners that the false teachings of the rapier have taken hold. Indeed, so increasingly popular was the new rapier practice that foreign teachers were much in demand during the last quarter of the century. We know that Rocco Bonetti, Jeronimo, and Vincentio Saviolo—as the most conspicuous foreign masters of this period—frequently traveled outside London to instruct their students. Silver wants to see such Italian teachers challenged to fencing displays before they can begin teaching in England. "They shall play with such weapons as they profess to teach withal, three bouts apiece with three of the best English Masters of Defence, and three bouts apiece with three unskillful valiant men, and three bouts apiece with three resolute men half-drunk. Then if they can defend themselves against these Masters of Defence, and hurt, and go free from the rest, then are they to be honored, cherished, and allowed for perfect good teachers, what country men soever they be" (Jackson 501).

On the surface, this might sound a reasonable trial by combat, no more difficult than most that were held at the time—assuming it was possible to find three drunkards who could fight. Although he assumed they would prefer using their beloved rapiers, it is a sign of Silver's confidence in the English sword that he allows the Italian teachers their choice of weapons. But the rapier was optimally designed—and Silver well knew this—to face off against another rapier. Rapier thrusts could be effective against English swords, but usually only in abbreviated combat. An Italian fighter would not choose an English style fighter as an opponent. A few hits against an English sword, particularly in a prolonged fight, would easily break or bend a rapier blade.

Silver knew, of course, that the Italian fencing teachers were unlikely to accept such a challenge. The influence of the Masters of Defense had fragmented since their original license (invalidated by the death of Henry VIII in 1547) had never been reapplied to a succeeding group. We do know that several fencing teachers had the patronage, however minimal, of certain nobility well into the seventeenth century. We also have some records of their meetings, if none of their curriculum.[3]

But there was no longer an effectively organized cartel of English Masters who could control the teaching and display of personal combat. It was probably not just Italian and Spanish fencing masters who were putting up their own shingles and attracting whatever kind of clientele they could. Certainly there must have been Englishmen (as well as Germans and Spaniards) who tried to cash in on the new movement.

Seen in this light, Silver's challenge remains not only of doubtful effectiveness, but seems a desperate attempt to intimidate the new foreign teachers of swordplay. Cultural history is full of examples of organizations, recognizing their declining influence, suddenly calling for standards and certification of all practitioners. Although such movements may be motivated partly out of a true concern and love for the discipline, also involved is the wish to preserve a hierarchically controlled and profitable way of living. Unions and professional organizations in our own day, in addition to regulation, also seek to protect their own, and this is not necessarily a cynical observation. The English Masters had had it their own way for decades. Their motivation and reaction is understandable. Silver wanted to press the issue the best way he could think of: contests with his cherished English weaponry resulting in the public humiliation and organized censure of the foreigners. At any rate, as far as we know the rapier teachers never accepted his challenge. But perhaps Silver at least gained a little face while the Italians might be called cowardly.

The Four Imperfections of Italian Swordplay

In their own country, when preparing for a fight, Italian fencers often wore gauntlets on their hands and mail under their shirts. Silver points out that the Italian masters frequently didn't mention this added defense to their English students, thus flagrantly misrepresenting their technique. His point is that if such protection is ever considered a part of rapier play, then the weapon is deficient in protection. The idea of a hidden shirt of mail would also bruise the English sense of fair play.

The rapier stylists, in their defense, would have said the gauntlets were a simple precaution—useful not only in real fighting, but a help in preventing accidental punctures or bruises in practice, particularly against an uncontrolled beginning student. The gauntlet went in and out of fashion as the rapier continued to develop in the seventeenth century. And as the rapier blade became continually less effective as a slashing weapon, a gentleman's glove might be all that was needed to guide the opponent's blade aside. Silver is trying to make something of it, but the fact remains that gauntlet wearing was usually a personal matter.

A second imperfection of Italian swordplay was the all-too-common double kill. There is sufficient anecdotal evidence in literary remains to suggest that Silver was not fabricating this fact. There was a great emphasis placed on aggressive thrusting action in the Italian style. As we have seen in Di Grassi and Saviolo, however, the best teachers emphasized, at minimum, voiding the body and concurrently countering the opponent's attack as one thing. A double slaying occurred when fighters lost proper distance and began to attack impetuously, even wildly. To be fair, double kills are symptomatic of the tense psychology of fighting and could happen with almost any kind of weapon.

Silver's third major objection to rapiers is that they come in such varied lengths that fight efficiency is lost. But this was hardly a problem unique to rapier play. There was no such thing as a standard sword length in Elizabethan England, as close inspection of swords in modern collections can attest. Swords and rapiers came in many different lengths, primarily depending on the strength, skill, and taste of the fencer. Hamlet's query in the duel scene is, therefore, more than a simple idle test of fairness. "These foils have all a length?" (V, ii, 254) would be the first question of a good fencer in Shakespeare's day.

Silver's point has unique application to the rapier however. It was certainly true that a rapier severely out of proportion to its owner was laughably ineffective, due to the weapon's supreme dependence on the efficiency of attack. A rapier too long for the fighter put him out of range, making attacks and retreats awkward. On the other hand, a rapier of insufficient length put the fighter in too close quarters. As we saw in Di Grassi's and Saviolo's works, a precise sense of distance—and therefore weapon balance—was a necessary aspect of successful rapier technique.

Ill-proportioned rapiers were common in Silver's day. If an extra inch or two of blade length gave the fighter the advantage, why not? Blade length alone might tip the fight balance to the less skilled fencer. More often, however, excessive blade length was simply gentlemanly affectation. Stow mentions that when it be-came the fashion to have long rapiers and long collars and cuffs—some an outlandish and unwieldy five to six feet long—Queen Elizabeth proclaimed that "selected grave citizens" would be placed at various city gates, "to cut the Ruffes and breake the Rapier's poynts of all passengers that exceeded a yeard in length of their rapier, and a nayle of a yard in depth of their ruffes" (Castle 21).

Silver's fourth point, that the hilts on most rapiers are insuffi-cient both for protecting the hands and for parrying, was only partly true. The rapier was never designed for true parrying in English sword style; the hilt design was intended to deflect an opponent's sword point. Italian teachers preferred simultaneous attacks or voiding procedures with the body. Parrying in a traditional (English sword) way with a rapier would not only be awkward and ineffective, but deadly.

Silver's objections to the Italian style are only moderately significant. Some confuse beginner's mistakes with polished technique, while others are symptomatic of the unpredictability of all dueling situations. All the objections are based on English sword fight assumptions.

The Six Chief Causes That Swordsmen May Be Killed by Men of Small Skill or None at All

Silver's startling claim is that for all its fancy footwork and arcane terminology, rapier swordplay cannot protect against even the most basic attacks. There are six causes of this.

First, the Italian swordsman does not keep the four Governors: judgment, distance, time, and place. As Silver explains:[4] Judgment is knowing that moment when your opponent can reach you or you can reach him. This is derived from training, experience, and knowledge of the opposing fighter's strengths and weaknesses. Distance refers to the space needed for defensive purposes and is a precise sense developed in the well-trained swordsman, letting him instantly adjust to the opponent's movements and thus preserving proper space (sometimes called the fencing measure) between fighters. Modern competitive fencers have developed this sense to a high degree. Kendo also places great stress on this idea of a buffer zone (known as *ma* or *ma-ai*). Silver says that the rapier specialist's sense of distance is distorted, since he must use the feet more extensively and must constantly seek to close for the attack. Once he has closed, he is momentarily vulnerable to the English swordsman's attack, which takes little or no footwork to execute.

To complete an attack or retreat obviously requires time. More precisely, the better fencer instantaneously calculates how much time it takes to reach the place of his opponent with his sword. This is based on knowing the opponent's reaction speed, tendencies, and style, combined with his own ability to meet or exceed those speeds and tendencies. For the English swordsman it means attack quickly and be ready to retreat quickly if the attack is not successful. The term place is somewhat unclear and is never exactly defined, but most probably refers to the fencer's body orientation vis-à-vis his opponent, and it is clearly a function of distance. Silver believes that the rapier fighter's time and place are distorted. Compared to the English swordsman, the rapier style does not allow for quick and safe retreat. This is due to the rapier's greater reliance on long distance attacks and the use of complex footwork.

A second cause of hurt is not observing the four Actions, called bent, spent, lying spent, and drawing back. Bent is a preparation for an attack; spent is the termination of an attack; lying spent is the pause after spent (a particular dangerous moment); and drawing back refers to the withdrawal of the weapon and/or the retreat, particularly emphasized by Silver. The four Actions, in other words, comprise a complete cycle from preparation for an attack to the final withdrawal of body and weapon. Creating such distinct phases is clearly the work of a swordsman, not a rapier specialist.

The third cause is that the fencer may not understand the best (true) times for attack. In the heat of a contest, many fencers take their opportunities by chance, not accurate judgment. The best movements are derived from the four Governors and the four Actions.

The fourth cause is the inability of the swordsman to respond to what Silver calls the variable fight; that is, an opponent who tries a wide variety of attacks and responses. This is sound advice, echoed by Di Grassi and Saviolo. Without doubt there were many arcane or odd techniques taught by other teachers. A good fighter had to expect the unexpected. The best way to reply to the variable fight would be to keep a prudent, constant distance and to wait for a quick opening or sudden advantage. Without such distance (acting as a kind of buffer zone) the variety of attacks and feints could be overwhelming, and the untrained fencer would fight back carelessly.

In addition, once rapier blades had crossed, there was a tendency for fighters—both skilled and otherwise—to finally close with their daggers. It was difficult to escape injury in such a situation.

Silver suggests that with short swords such a moment would be rare. Distance, timing, and logical parries in a true English combat would eliminate such messy encounters.

Fifth, a rapier fighter's blade is so long that he must retreat with the feet after crossing weapons with the opponent. Silver counts this a liability since it takes longer to move the feet than to simply retract the sword and strike again, as the English sword allows.

The sixth cause is that many rapiers are too heavy to use in proper time. Remembering that many long-bladed rapiers were dangerously out of balance, we can understand his meaning of too heavy.

The Deceptions of Italian Teachers

Silver says that the Italian schoolmasters deceive their English students. First, their teaching is not based on the Governors or Actions described above. Second, rapier play is most effective as a classroom exercise, undertaken in the gentlemanly confines of the fencing hall. Actual combat is quicker and rougher than this. Third, the unskilled student cannot accurately judge what kind of teaching he is getting.

Silver's most serious charge, that rapier play is technically unsound, is demonstrated with an example. He cites the case of two ship captains who began to quarrel on the quay, finally drawing rapiers. They had both been taught that the attacker always had the advantage. With hardly a hesitation, and with great force and speed they rushed headlong, simultaneously slaying each other.

When a rapier fighter faced an opponent who, like himself, was taught the value of always lying in defensive ward, the result seemed even more ridiculous, though sometimes less fatal. In such a case, they "with all speed . . . put themselves in ward . . . and thereupon they stand sure, saying the one to the other, thrust and thou dare; and says the other, thrust and thou dare, or strike or thrust and thou dare, says the other; then says the other, strike and thrust and thou dare for thy life" (Jackson 506). Eventually each discovers a way to retire, ego intact, without delivering a blow, much as the cautious Touchstone relates: "I durst go no further than the Lie Circumstantial, nor he durst not give me the

Lie Direct; and so we measured swords and parted" (*As You Like It*, V, iv, 80–82).

But even placed as opposing strategies these techniques are unlikely to be successful. The fencer trained to aggressively thrust at all times is often out of proper distance and may find himself having thrust without crossing distance between fighters. He is out of balance and time and is easily killed. The defender merely has to redirect the point of his blade, with a turn of the wrist, at the attacker's face or body as he charges. The constant defender, on the other hand, neither seizes the opportunities given him by a zealous opponent, nor creates advantages through well-chosen attacks. Silver finds this all out of keeping, and easily remedied, with his four Governors.

Silver ultimately answers the question of who has the advantage, the attacker or defender, by saying neither do—and both do. "That is, whosoever wins or gains the place in true pace, space and time has the advantage, whether he is striker, thruster, or warder" (Jackson 511). He means, of course, that the best strategy in fighting is to rely on relative circumstances, not to slavishly apply only one kind of tactic to all situations. In this, he is quite close to Di Grassi and Saviolo in championing a flexible, but disciplined, response.

As we read *Paradoxes* it becomes clear that Silver is not interested in discussing theoretical considerations or elegant classroom forms. He is talking about techniques drawn from real fights he has seen and heard. And real fights, unlike the classroom variety, have higher stakes, putting inordinate pressure on fighters to respond quickly. According to Silver, winning and losing within the rapier systems are more frequently the result of accidental forces and not smart swordplay.

Perhaps Silver is too quick to condemn Italian-style swordplay for what is, finally, the most common and predictable reaction to combat throughout history. A highly trained and experienced fighter can show some control and discipline, even when things go wrong. But most fighters are not cool under pressure. Some modern military studies suggest that the majority of all firepower in a battle is not aimed at the enemy. Modern weaponry makes it very easy to spray bullets without being precise.

The parallel to Elizabethan rapier swordplay is acute, though the technology is clearly not as complicated. Compared to what had come before—contrasted to such as the hand-and-a-half or bastard sword, the English short sword, the axe, and so forth—rapier design radically changed the kind of timing and necessary risk inherent in dueling. Working within a much narrower range of attack, with the point and not the edge of the blade, the slightest of tactical errors in judgment might mean the end. In such a high-stakes situation, the stress is enormous, and the pressure to do something—anything—and to do it before the opponent does something else is overwhelming. Few men are strong enough to be patient in a real sword fight. The skills used in practice are frequently forgotten. Imagine the tension of a western gunfight, but at a distance of six to eight feet, and you get something of the feel of this situation.[5]

The Italian masters probably would not have had a serious quarrel with this criticism. Fighting can really be learned only by doing. Exercises and classroom discipline merely shadow the reality. It was a combination of forces—the new rapier play, more weapons available, varying expertise in training, a greater willing-ness to settle scores by dueling, and so forth—that opened up new violent ways between men. The relative speedup in rapier fighting precipitated much new uncertainty and danger. The old notions of time and distance were replaced by rapier strategy. There might often be unnecessarily dangerous encounters until the new weap-on's requirements were more firmly established and practiced. But to an Englishman like Silver, this was nothing short of a break-down in the traditional rules of engagement that must have seemed not only chaotically dangerous, but unsporting.

Of Spanish Fighters

Spanish fighters were known for their elegant, though sometimes arcane, style of rapier play (see chapters 1 and 3). According to Silver, this meant "stand[ing] as brave as they can with their bodies straight upright, narrow spaced, with their feet continually moving, as if they were in a dance, holding forth their arms and rapiers very straight against the face or body of their enemy"

(Jackson 512). Silver says that this is a fine theory, as long as the rapier can be held with its point straight at the opponent—not an easy thing given its often over-long and heavy design. One slight misstep opens the Spaniard to injury, with no defensive reactions left in reserve.

He cites an example also used by Shakespeare in *Romeo and Juliet*. There was a much-discussed contemporary story of an Italian teacher of defense (Rocco Bonetti) who was reputed to be so excellent in his fighting technique that "he would have hit any Englishman with a thrust, just upon any button in his doublet" (Jackson 514). Mercutio refers to Tybalt as "the very butcher of a silk button, a duellist, a duellist!" (II, iv, 23–24). Such tales encouraged adulation of the Italian fencing technique. Silver, like Mercutio, doubts such fine technique can be attained, let alone taught to others.[6]

A Proof That the Blow Is Swifter Than the Thrust

In one of the most famous passages of false reasoning in the history of swordplay, Silver attempts to prove that the arc of a blow is equidistant to a thrust: "Let two lie in their perfect strengths and readiness, wherein the blades of their rapiers by the motion of the body, may not be crossed of either side, the one to strike, and the other to thrust. Then measure the distance or course wherein the hand and hilt pass to finish the blow of the one, and the thrust of the other, and you shall find them both by measure, in distance all one" (Jackson 516).

In the very next section, however, Silver modifies his antagonism. "There is no fight perfect without both blow and thrust: neither is there any certain rule to be set down for the use of the point only" (Jackson 517). Here we arrive at the heart of Silver's objections to the rapier style of play. Most fighting, Silver contends, is what he would call variable or variant, that is, consisting of a wide variety of hand, arm, body, and foot motions. To rely on just one style of attack is unnecessarily restrictive. A fighter should be ready to thrust, or blow, or void the body, or give ground. Sometimes a fighter should be aggressive, sometimes defensive, and so forth.

In a later section entitled "Of evil orders or customs in our English Fence-Schools," Silver extends his argument for variable fighting prowess at some length. For example:

> If the thrust be best, why do we not use it at the single Sword, Sword & Dagger, & Sword and Buckler? If the blow be best, why do we not use it at the single rapier, rapier & Poiniard? But knowing by the Art of Arms, that no fight is perfect without both blow and thrust, why do we not use and teach both blow and thrust?. . .Surely, I think a downright fellow, that never came in school, using such skill as nature yields out of his courage, strength, and agility, with good downright blows and thrusts among, as shall best frame in his hands, should put one of these imperfect scholars greatly to his shifts. Besides, there are now in these days no grips, closes, wrestlings, striking with the hilts, daggers, or bucklers, used in Fence schools. Our ploughmen by nature will do all these things with great strength and agility, but the Schoolman is altogether unacquainted with these things . . . being fast tied to such school-play as he has learned, has lost thereby the benefit of nature, and the plowman is now by nature without art a far better man than he. Therefore, in my opinion, *as long as we bar any manner of play in school, we shall hardly make a good scholar* . . . [for this was] the ancient teaching (emphasis added). (Jackson 522)

Although there is practical truth to his interest in adaptable and variable fighting technique, Silver's primary objections are exemplary of that kind of conservative chauvinism which places great emphasis on the old ways, the traditional practices of a discipline, even, as above, using the primitive as an example of untutored skill.[7] In the rapier, Silver saw a threat, not an evolution.

We can indeed be sure that many fights at this time—as in most times—did not have probable outcomes. It sometimes happens that even the well-trained, experienced fighter may be bested by a beginner, what Silver means by the downright fellow. By concentrating on real-life possibilities, he sought to demonstrate a lack of fundamental dependability in the new rapier style. Unfortunately for the fighter—even the expert—there are many variables that can throw off or negate hard-earned training and planning. Sir Thomas Overbury's contention that it was hard to find a fight master of the time who still had both eyes contains a grain of truth (Aylward, *The English Master of Arms* 36).

Silver emphasizes the greater violence of blows when compared to thrusts. "The force of a thrust passes straight, therefore any cross [parry] being indirectly made, the force of a child may put it by: but the force of a blow passes indirectly, therefore must be directly warded in the countercheck of his force" (Jackson 519). In addition, a thrust may not stop an opponent quickly enough: "I have known a Gentleman hurt in rapier fight, in nine or ten places through the body, arms and legs, and yet hath continued in his fight, & afterward slain the other" (Jackson 519). Compare this to a blow with a good, stout English blade, which severs arms, legs, or even head completely.

The most frequent cause of death from dueling was not the immediate kill from either blow or thrust; it was death by blood loss or from infection. This could occur long after the fight was over. (Actually, the out-and-out kill was rare—exciting dueling stories notwithstanding.) Casually dismissing rapier puncture wounds that introduced massive internal infections and bleeding is misleading on Silver's part.

Comparing the True Fight to the False

Silver contends that in good fight technique the hand moves before the feet. Conversely, moving the feet before the hand should be avoided. As he explains it: "Whatsoever is done with the foot or feet before the hand, is false, because the hand is swifter than the foot, the foot or feet being a slower mover than the hand. The hand in that manner of fight is tied to the time of the foot or feet, and being tied thereto, has lost its freedom, and is made thereby as slow in his motions as the foot or feet; therefore that fight is false" (Jackson 521).

As we have noted in Di Grassi and Saviolo, body voiding maneuvers were commonly taught by the rapier stylists as a necessary adjunct to the movements of the weapon. This could be confusing to an Englishman brought up on the English sword style. Silver ignores two points: (1) the Italian masters' insistence on moving the feet was always accompanied by specific weapon counterattacks; it was not as if the feet moved in isolation from weapon movement, and (2) since the rapier depended on body positioning that easily led to thrusting attacks, this gave the rapier man more time to defend the body by voiding maneuvers. Incorporating the blow with excessive footwork—thus creating variable spacing between opponents—would indeed be too slow. But this is an attempt to create an awkward hybrid of rapier and English sword styles.

The Principles of True Fight
with All Manner of Weapons

Silver says that all single weapons have four wards: two with the point up and two with the point down. We may assume he means that all areas from the shoulder and neck down to the thigh and knee may be protected using these four wards.

He uses sword and buckler, and sword and dagger as examples of double weapons. For these there are eight wards: two with the point up, two with point down, two for the legs with point down (with knuckles downward), and two for dagger or buckler that protect the head. Notice that Silver increases the number of parrying options Di Grassi describes. This for him is a logical derivation from the standard single sword technique of strong parry, without regard for immediate counterattack. For this reason, the number of parries proliferates, becoming an end in itself. This is a core distinction between earlier sixteenth century sword style and the new rapier technique introduced to England by such masters as Di Grassi and Saviolo.

Silver then describes the eight times, by which he means the sequence of physical actions that may be used to initiate attack or defense. A true time will always start with the hand moving, then may be added the body, then body and one foot, and finally body and both feet. As he has already stated, the action of the hand is easiest to initiate. This is in opposition to Di Grassi's and Saviolo's injunctions which require simultaneous foot and body movements.

Silver says that false time will be initiated by the foot, or foot and body, or foot, body, and hand, or both feet, body, and hand. Speculating on the differences in relative speed between these two kinds of fights, we see that a true fight for Silver could be quite deliberate and slow, the two fighters taking solid positions and defending them. One can imagine knights in armor fighting in this style. This technical stance links Silver to the old ways and means of English fighters.

A false fight, on the other hand—that is, one based on Di Grassi and Saviolo—would be more varied in its use of stance, torso movement, and angles of attack. This is easy enough to see in the illustrations from Di Grassi and Saviolo (and of Agrippa and Capo Ferro in their works). It would also more likely be a faster fight. By fast we do not mean anything like modern competitive fencing (see chapter 5). There would still be, in the false rapier fight, a great sense of phrasing and distinction between each separate attack and defense.

Silver then demonstrates the ideal length of the sword (Figure 11). "To know the perfect length of your Sword, you shall stand with your sword and dagger drawn, as you see this picture, keeping out straight your dagger arm, drawing back your sword as far as conveniently you can, not opening the elbow joint of your sword arm, and look what you can draw within your dagger, that is the just length of your sword, to be made according to your own stature. The perfect length of your two-hand sword is, the blade to be the length of the blade of your single sword " (Jackson 526–27).

By carefully examining Silver's picture, we may draw some interesting implications for his style of fight (see Figure 11). Note the upright posture and the widely spaced feet, solidly in contact with the ground. The knees are only modestly bent. The sword hand is well pulled back, already cocked to hit the enemy. No attempt is made to annoy the opponent with the sword tip in his face. The dagger is held far from the body, providing a deep cushion before the body. The whole attitude of the fighter seems settled, making him slower to move from his position.

This physical attitude would lend itself well to battle use, when hand to hand fighting became quite circumscribed and chaotic.

If the sword be longer, you can hardly vncrosse without going backe with your feet. If shorter, tho you can hardly make a true crosse without putting in of your feet, the which times are too long to answer the time of the hand.

The like reasons for the short staffe, half Pike, Forrest bill, Partisan, or Gleue, or such like weapons of perfect length.

Figure 11. The sole illustration from Silver's manual, showing the determination of the perfect length of a sword. The right hand is comfortably retracted and the dagger hand is gently stretched forward. (By permission of the Folger Shakespeare Library)

Silver reemphasizes that the rapier is utterly worthless in such situations, but the short sword is ideal:

> The short Sword, and Sword and dagger, are perfect good weapons, and especially in service of the Prince. What a brave weapon is a short sharp light Sword, to carry, to draw, to be nimble withal, to strike, to cut, to thrust both strong and quick. And what a good defence is a strong single hilt, when men are clustering and hurling together, especially where variety of weapons be, in their motions to defend the hand, head, face, and bodies, from blows . . . given sometimes with swords, sometimes with two-handed swords, battle Axe, Hal-

berds, or black Bills, and sometimes men shall be so near together that they shall have no space, scarce to use the blades of their Swords below their waists. . . . Then they lay on, [using] blows and grips. One valiant man with a Sword in his hand, will do better service, than ten *Italians*, or Italianated with the Rapiers. (Jackson 531)

The advantages of the English sword in war fit nobly with Silver's traditional approach to weaponry. A weapon like the short sword, a classic of English history, had shown its worth through centuries of use. But Silver surely knew that Di Grassi and Saviolo were not proselytizing the rapier for battle; there is no direct reference in either Italian's work to use in war. The rapier was designed for more personal battles: the wars of honor, reputation, and ego. And as has been discussed, even the hallowed short sword was of less and less value in late sixteenth-century battlefields fundamentally transformed by the use of gunpowder, pike, and bow.

Although Silver's pleas are out of date, even laughable in some instances, reading his romantic attachment to the old ways is oddly charming. Was this the argument of an old warhorse, proud of his record, but bitter at the new ways of combat? Or was it an English fencing expert's calculated attack on unwanted foreign influence, written primarily to retain his own reputation? Without any more personal history we may never know the answer.

Further Technical Notes on Rapier vs. Short Sword

In addition to more fundamental inequities of the rapier vs. the sword, Silver also finds fault with the common partner weapons that go with each: the dagger (or poniard) with the rapier, and the buckler with the sword. He doesn't dismiss the use of the dagger, especially with a good sword, but it is clear that he finds the buckler much more versatile and safer to use.

Against another rapier, of course, as we have seen in Di Grassi and Saviolo, direct blocking parries would have been altogether rare, since primary attacks are thrusts. A rapier man's main defensive action against thrusts was the body void, accompanied by light dagger parries. A rapier specialist parrying against a sword, however, would have been an entirely different thing, awkwardly pitting the light, precise rapier play against a swinging sword. To accurately place a dagger for parries against a sword would require enormous confidence on the part of the rapier man. A blade only twelve to fifteen inches long would carry little blocking power. In addition, the necessary timing and distance a rapier specialist required would seriously distort the dagger's placement to the incoming sword attack.

The authors have experimented defending cutting attacks with daggers, and we can assure the reader that only the bravest of fencers can utilize the dagger for parries in such situations. It is usually preferable, particularly in multiple attacks, to use rapier parries with simultaneous body voids instead of solitary dagger moves. A rapier/dagger against a good short sword would be extremely dangerous. The rapier man would not want to seek direct blocking moves, but would stay out of reach and try to dart in when possible.

The buckler, on the other hand, can defend against a wide variety of attacks, both thrusts and blows, and this gives it an enormous advantage over the dagger. In addition, by virtue of hand speed (and also due to its greater surface area that forgives slight inaccuracies), the buckler can cover wider areas. Here Silver recalls his rule about the hand being quicker than the feet: "the hand is the swiftest motion, the foot is the slowest, without distance the hand is tied to the motion of the feet, whereby the time of the hand is made as slow as the foot" (Jackson 534).

In close quarters, a buckler can more efficiently defend or strike since the buckler man merely moves his hands quickly while separating his defense (parry) from the offense (cut). The rapier fighter, contrarily, must constantly shift his feet in short distance, with little time, in addition to using simultaneous parries and thrusts. This is quite dangerous in a fight with a swordsman. "So those that trust to their fight, the excellency of a good eye, their great cunning, & perfect wards of the daggers, that they can better see to ward than with a buckler, shall ever be deceived" (Jackson 535).

In this special case of rapier against sword, Silver's confidence in the buckler seems well-placed, although by his time, the use of sword and buckler was seen as a particularly lower-class or servant's weapon. For instance, Shakespeare's use of a sword and buckler fight in the first scene of *Romeo and Juliet* was intended to show the difference in fight styles between servants and upper-class characters such as Tybalt and Mercutio who sport rapiers. Buckler fighting can be noisy, and close-in tactics such as wrestling, tripping, and grappling make it look less elegant than the upper-class rapier fights. The effect in Shakespeare's first scene, therefore, in addition to its excitement, would have been comic to his audiences. Also, in *Henry IV, Part 1*, Hotspur refers derogatorily to Hal as "that same sword-and-buckler Prince of Wales" (I, iii, 229). Shakespeare expects his audience to understand the intended slight of such a comment in reference to royalty. Based on the evidence we have, it is apparent that the short sword and buckler, valuable as they may have been in earlier times, were devolving into weapons of the lower classes that elicited scorn and laughter.

Fighting Between Men of Various Statures and Physical Skills

In a conversation between a master and his student (much like Saviolo's style) Silver demonstrates how the tall man will almost always have the advantage over a shorter man, even though both are well-trained. Just as in boxing, the longer reach and stride tilt the odds to the taller fighter.[8] Silver does say, however, that the shorter man can derive some advantage by foot movements, through "progression, regression, traversing, and treading of grounds. In any of these you play the part of the Patient, or Patient Agent [that is, being on the defensive]. Because his weight and number of his feet in his coming to win the true place to strike or thrust home, are greater than yours, and therefore the true time is yours to avoid him, or safely defend yourself" (Jackson 544).

Silver then develops a number of fighter/skill combinations with the most likely outcomes. For instance, if two men have skill at rapier, it frequently falls out that they close very quickly, where grappling and wrestling techniques (this is Silver's preference) may be the only options. In this case, the stronger wrestler wins the match. Silver points out that due to the rapier's extreme length, if one of the fighters wishes to run in quickly, he will have the advantage since it is easier to run forward in attack than backward in defense. Once proper distance is closed, however, the rapiers are useless.

If we may believe Silver's description of the garden-variety rapier fight, it was often the case—as we have said before—that both fighters would be injured or slain. The key to rapier fighting is on the quick attack. Distance must be closed only enough to thrust home. "And this is well known unto all men of skill, that the place [distance] being once gotten, there is neither judgment, space, pace, nor time, either by wards with their rapier blades, or by breaking with the Poiniards, or flying back, that can preserve or defend them" (Jackson 547). Then the final thrusts were frequently made with the daggers.

In a brief section which analyzes not only technique, but also fight psychology, Silver reveals how a man of no skill can win:

> He that hath no skill most commonly proves himself the better man, for these causes or reasons following. First the skillful man as knowing the other to have no skill, or finding it to be so by his shape or manner of coming towards him, will presently yield to take the advantage of his coming, or else with all speed put himself into his short ward, to be ready at his coming to make out a strong *Stoccatta* (as the *Italians* call it). The other, knowing his imperfection in fight, assures himself there can be no great good for him to stand long out at the point, [so] presently redoubles or revives his spirits with perfect resolution, to make short work, courageously with some offensive action . . . flies in with all force and agility. The skillful man stands watching to take such advantages as his schoolmaster has taught him, in the which time, many times it falls out, he is taught a new time, even by an unskillful man . . . is therefore hurt or slain. And if . . . they both miss in their offensive actions, then by reason thereof, and of the imperfect length of their rapiers, they come to stabbing with their Poiniards, wherein there lies no defense, because distance being broken, judgment fails, time is lost, and their eyes (by the swift motions of their hands) are deceived. (Jackson 547–48)

A fight between two unskilled men with rapiers often ends up being a dagger fight.

Of the Imperfection and Insufficiency of the Fight of the Single Rapier, Rapier and Poniard, Rapier and Buckler, Rapier and Cloak, and Rapier and Glove of Mail

In his summing up of the *Paradoxes*, Silver repeats his major disagreements with the rapier stylists:

1. True fight may involve four different situations[9]: (a) the gardant fight: that is, holding the sword hilt above the head with point down; (b) the open fight: hilt is held above the head, point upright or backwards; (c) the close fight: when both swords cross, points down or up; this may also occur when the space is narrow and swords are not crossed; (d) the variable fight: all other guards not covered above, including[10]

   —*Stoccata,* right leg forward, hilt held to side of right thigh, dagger held point up, point of sword behind dagger point if possible.

   —*Imbroccata,* point of sword held wide and under the level of dagger point.

   —*Mountanta,* raising the hilt from low side to overhead to make a quick thrust at face or chest of opponent.

   —*Passata,* thrusting both dagger and sword points at opponent, sword held to enemy's belly.

2. A weapon that cannot be used in all four styles is unsafe. The rapier is effective only in variable and close fights.

3. The rapier lacks a proper hilt to protect the hand.

4. The rapier cannot parry head and shoulder cuts effectively.

5. Adding other instruments, such as poniard, buckler, or mail glove does not solve these basic deficiencies, since they are most effective in the fight styles the rapier is weakest at, namely the variable and close fight modes.

Now that we have discussed Silver's use of such terms as time, distance, and gardant, we can best understand his famous broadside:

Now, O you Italian teachers of Defense, where are your *Stocca-tas, Imbroccatas, Mandrittas, Puntas, & Punta Riversas, Strami-sons, Passatas, Carricados, Amazzas, & Incartatas,* & playing with your bodies, removing with your feet a little aside, circle wise winding of your bodies, making of three times with your feet together, marking with one eye the motion of the adversary, & with the other eye the advantage of thrusting? What is become of all these juggling gambolds, Apish devices, with all the rest of your squint-eyed tricks, when as through your deep studies, long practices, & apt bodies, both strong and agile, you have attained to the height of all these things? What then avails it you, when you shall come to fight for your lives with a man of skill? You shall have neither time, nor place, in due time to perform any one of them, nor gardant nor open fight safely to keep out a man of skill, a man of no skill, or scholar of your own teaching, from the true place, the place of safety, the place of uncertainty or mischief, the place of wounds or death, but are there enforced to stand in that mischievous, uncertain, dangerous, and most deadly place, as two men having lost in part their chiefest senses, most furiously with their rapiers or poniards, wounding or slaying each other. (Jackson 553)

Of as much concern to Silver as the inefficiency of rapier techniques in real fighting was his sorrow at seeing the art of defense becoming the art of picking quarrels. As we have cited in previous chapters, the late sixteenth century saw a significant rise in the rate of private quarrels, among all classes. Saviolo's *Of Honor and Honourable Quarrels* is one of the most famous written treatises that deals with this development and accepts the reality of dueling, seeking only to control its form.

Silver takes a slightly different tack on this. He says—contrary to the evidence we have—that the total amount of fighting decreased, the rapier being so unreliable that many men simply backed off from confrontations. However, Silver says among the gentlemen who used it, a greater percentage were injured or killed. "They have made many a strong man in his fight weak, many a valiant man fearful, many a worthy man trusting to their imperfect fight, has been slain" (Jackson 555). Silver adds sadly that even the death of the Italian fencing masters will not see the end of this terrible carnage. Left in their wake are "false Fence books, imperfect weapons, false fights, and evil customs, whereby for lack of use and practice in perfect weapons and true fight, we are disabled for the service of our Prince, defense of our country, and safety of our lives in private fight" (Jackson 555).

For George Silver, rapier fighting was no less than the evisceration of all manly English fighting. The paradox of Elizabethan swordplay that he refers to lay in the growing popularity of the Italian style, weakening England's very ability to defend itself against its enemies while at the same time encouraging the citizenry to fight among themselves over petty points of conduct. As a traditional English fencer anxious to turn back the tide, Silver exhorts his countrymen to preserve the old ways.

But for many reasons such a past could never be regained. Once a new technology and its accompanying human behavior have made inroads, reversal is unlikely. The rapier was a compelling change in personal defense for which the time had come.

5
Elizabethan Swordplay
Reconstructed

IN THE PRECEDING chapters we have described and analyzed the work of three fencing experts in England from the Elizabethan period. There are significant differences among them, but some constants may be gleaned from their writings. In this chapter, we attempt to bring together the variety of ideas we have discussed in order to create a standard fighting style: a typical Elizabethan rapier style, if you will, with the understanding that significant portions of what we are about to describe are not only derived from our theoretical understanding of the texts, but are also based on our years of experience as fencers, stage fighters, and fight choreographers.

This reconstruction is also intended to assist the theatrical director and fight choreographer in achieving the highest degree of historical accuracy in rapier fights. By using our outline of a standard fight style, a choreographer can quickly verify whether his work contains the prototypical elements for Elizabethan period fighting. It is not our intention, of course, to restrict the creation of newer and possibly more theatrical and modern movements. That is the difference between the historical methods and practice and the modern art of theatre. We simply offer these insights as a way to widen the possible choices available to the choreographer and director in their search for more exciting and effective fight scenes. For the scholar, this chapter—coupled with the historical information in the rest of this book—should serve as a beginning guide to deciphering elements of swordplay as they arise in Elizabethan literature.

We've seen how an apparently simple physical act like fighting may be broken down into dozens of elements, each one crucial in preserving the difference between life and death. In choosing elements to emphasize, we have eliminated specialized, complicated, or idiosyncratic maneuvers. Though such unusual techniques were used historically, they are too arcane for our purposes. We are trying to describe Elizabethan rapier swordplay in its most characteristic form, not attempting to account for every possible personal variation. This chapter, therefore, constructs an icon of Elizabethan rapier swordplay; within its design, virtually all elements of rapier play can be understood and applied.

With this caveat in mind, we can broadly separate the various aspects of good rapier swordplay into the following categories: stance, footwork, sense of space, timing and rhythm, offensive maneuvers, defensive maneuvers, and strategy.

Stance

The modern fencing stance consisting of wide base, feet well apart, knees bent, front foot pointed to the opponent, and body turned sideways to the enemy with the empty hand held relaxed next to the back of the head is a widely recognized image of fencing in our day. The rapier, however, demanded a different physical orientation to the opponent. Di Grassi's text and figures, for example, show relatively upright bodies. The distance between fighters seems quite close; a simple thrust with the rapier is easily executed without much torso inclining or long striding. The rapier fighters also face each other more directly.

Saviolo incorporates a slightly more open style of stance . If we study the pictures in his text, we note wider bases than Di Grassi shows. Saviolo's fencers seem more alert, primed for quick footwork, front and back. The fencer's rear heel in Saviolo's pictures is often raised, implying weight shifts. The unarmed hand is also more clearly used in a defensive posture; the fighter seems prepared to sacrifice the left arm in order to deflect any attack that can't be parried in time with the rapier.

Silver's stances —and here we must make some reference to his *Bref Instructions* for detailed physical movements—look more like Di Grassi's with a narrower base, on flat feet. As we have seen, the Englishman Silver has very little patience with sticking and thrusting. He prefers a stance that is much more up-front, willing to stand its ground. Despite this close-fighting orientation how-

ever, Silver carefully points out that the fighter must be prepared
to retreat quickly after an attack.

All our experts agree that one foot must be placed forward. In
this position, the fencer can, with balance and vigor, thrust the
rapier forward, and at the same time can make quicker lateral
movements. This is not, however, anything like a modern, classical
fencing position in which the front foot is placed so far forward
that the knees must bend significantly. Our masters do not attempt
to attain the high-centered, elegant line of later seventeenth- and
eighteenth-century swordplay.

In addition, none of these texts indicate that rotating the torso
to either side—thus presenting a very narrow body target to the
opponent—was standard practice. There is probably one overrid-
ing significant reason for this: the use of a second weapon, usually
a dagger. In order to be effectively used as a parrying or, occasionally, a thrusting weapon, the dagger would have to be placed
forward, necessitating a more squared-off look to the torso. Because there is a wider body target, body voiding maneuvers in
which the feet and torso slide to one side or the other of the
attacking blade are used.

We believe that the most typical fighting stance for the rapier
in this period would look very much like a modern boxer's pose,
with the addition of the weapon, of course, and a slight forward
extension of the arms. Whatever their attempts at a more dignified
or upright posture at the beginning of a fight, given the nature of
the rapier thrust and the active intention of looking for an opening
in the opponent's guard, two Elizabethan fighters would very
quickly settle into a street-fighter mode: torso slightly collapsed,
one foot ahead of the other, rapier extended moderately in the
direction of the opponent with the point of the blade leading. The
other arm is ready to parry with the dagger or, in the case of the
single rapier, to help body balance when the weapon is extended
and the body begins to lean.

Footwork

One of the most distinctive aspects of any form of swordplay is
footwork. The medieval knights, for example, relying on armor to
protect them, would not have used intricate foot movement. It

seems almost comic to imagine a fully armored knight crossing one foot over the other, or traversing laterally. Indeed, the very design of full-armor joint articulations would have made these movements impossible.

In contrast, the Elizabethan fencers have described a wide variety of methods to advance the point of the rapier effectively. Footwork is integral to discovering the opening in the opponent's guard. This would mean a wide variety of steps, as we have discussed: paces forward and backward, lateral steps (the traverse), steps both small and large, stutter steps, even rocking the weight back and forth between feet without raising them off the ground.

Although the Elizabethans did not use what we would call a lunge—weapon arm fully extended, front foot stepping through so far that the front knee joint forms an angle of 90 degrees, the rear leg straight, and the body turned sideways to the opponent with the rear (empty) hand extended for balance behind—the rapier could be effective only with some sort of stride that brought the attack to the opponent.

All three masters describe moderate footsteps to assist rapier thrusts. Di Grassi asks for a "reasonable pace . . . if he would step forward to strike, he lengthen or increase one foot" (Jackson 30). Saviolo urges that the rear foot be ready and nimble, "as though he were to perform some feat of activity" (Jackson 212). Silver believes that all footwork must follow the motion of the sword and not precede it. Taken as a whole, these masters prefer relatively narrow bases and simple steps.

We have spoken previously of traverses, slips, and passes as the three basic kinds of steps. Instead of a lunge, an Elizabethan fighter would step (or often run) at the opponent, simply moving left-right-left-right, etc. This is a pass, where one foot passes the other, moving the body forward or backward. A traverse is a step to the side, either perpendicular or oblique to the forward line of attack. A slip is usually described as a small circular step backward and a bit to the outside with either foot, allowing the fighter to angle the body out of line, very effective in defensive maneuvers. These techniques would be significant characteristics of footwork for reconstructing rapier swordplay for the modern stage.

Sense of Space

Elizabethan fighters would have tended to move circularly, looking
for an opening to the left or right of the opponent. If we remember
the modern analogy of boxing, rapier swordplay movement patterns can easily be visualized. The occasional direct attack was
nearly always accompanied by an evasion of the body. We imagine
some ducking, bobbing, and weaving in these fights, much like
that performed by skilled modern boxers in the ring.

With the addition of daggers or cloaks to the single rapier (we
see these as sophisticated fight elements, occurring with more
regularity later in the time period), there would likely be an increase in frontal attacks. Taking on some of the function of the
shield, daggers and cloaks would close up the space between fighters. Cloaks and daggers would form the center of the circling
fighters, with the duelists moving on the circumference, swords
retracted slightly, eager to punch across the opponent's guard. The
image recalls that of circling dogs or fighting cocks.

Seen from without, rapier fighting was circular in nature. But
from the fighter's point of view, although movement easily slipped
to one side or the other in an attempt to find a good angle, when
initiating an attack, the Elizabethan rapier fighter would narrow
his vision. If we understand the kind of blade angles and simultaneous defense/attack maneuvers that Di Grassi and Saviolo recommend, duelists would feel themselves to be at both ends of a tube
of space. In our time, it could be compared to looking down the
barrel of your gun as your opponent looked down his. Medieval
swordplay must have seemed much broader and wider, with a
sense of expanding space to left, right, and overhead when cutting
and swinging with the heavier sword.

For an accomplished fencer, this restricted image of the fighting
zone in rapier play emphasized sighting the opponent's rapier
point and body. Either element might tip off the next possible
move. In modern psychological terms, this meant that the fencer
shifted constantly from a soft (general, overall) focus that allowed
him to see the opponent's entire figure in depth, to a narrow focus
that targeted the opponent's rapier point or hand movements.

Body voiding maneuvers are also part of a fighter's sense of space. Each of the masters taught some method to accomplish this. Here again, the kinesthetic differences in using the Elizabethan fighter's rapier and the medieval fighter's sword must have seemed enormous. Keeping in mind the relative weight, size, and manner of wielding each weapon, the knight moved more as a unit, consolidating his body behind each blow. The rapier fighter, on the other hand, moved more like a dancer: rotating, pivoting, lowering, and swinging his torso in time to the flow of attack. Ultimately, short sword fencing of the eighteenth century (which also saw the development of the modern ballet and was undoubtedly influenced by its use of body and space) would take this art of sword ballet to its highest levels.

Timing and Rhythm

The medieval fight (often described as bish-bash-bosh by fight choreographers) was singularly heavy and insistent in its rhythms. Little attempt was made to vary effort between strikes. A knight might try clusters of hits, but the old phrase, "they traded blows," is particularly meaningful to old swordplay. Due to the weight of armor and weapons, true heavy sword fights quickly wound down, leaving two gasping, straining knights attempting desperate single blows. This is why the phrase "they leaned for a while on their swords" is so common in medieval fight tales. As the knightly sword fight wore on, there was typically less time spent in actual fighting. See, for instance, Hotspur's descriptions of battle and the Glendower and Mortimer fight in *King Henry IV, Part 1* (I, iii, 30–32): "But I remember when the fight was done,/ When I was dry with rage and extreme toil,/ Breathless and faint, leaning upon my sword," and (98–103): "When on the gentle Severn's sedgy bank,/ In single opposition hand to hand,/ He did confound the best part of an hour/ In changing hardiment with great Glendower./ Three times they breathed, and three times did they drink, / Upon agreement, of swift Severn's flood."

The tempo of a rapier fight, in contrast to the medieval fight, was much lighter and quicker. Rest periods were a tradition that died out with the heavier swords. Rapier fights depended less on strength and more on quickness and accuracy. There are numerous examples of rapier fights ending within the first few exchanges. Many modern choreographed sword fights for productions of *Romeo and Juliet* ignore Benvolio's statement: "And to't they go like lightning; for, *ere I / Could draw to part them,* was stout Tybalt slain" (emphasis added) (III, i, 170–71). But between experts skilled at its cat and mouse techniques, a fight might last for some minutes.

Explosive in nature and relying less on the number of thrusts than on the right thrust, a typical rapier fight would have a wide variety of rhythmic possibilities: the quick extension parried with a clang of the dagger; the whooshing flip of a cloak; shoes sliding through the dust or on stones; the ring of the weapons momentarily parrying and sliding past each other. The rhythms of an Elizabethan fight, in other words, mirrored the rhythms of Elizabethan music in its use of syncopation, variety, and danceability. Comparing the fight style of the Elizabethan rapier expert to the medieval knight is like contrasting the tempo of the madrigal to Gregorian chants. Or using another musical metaphor, two rapier fighters are like a concerto (also devised at this time) in which the various instruments and melodies strike against each other. Is it any wonder that most of us see the rapier fight as a supreme example of romantic and flamboyant swordplay?

Of course, these are ideals. It must be admitted that with any but the top swordsmen of the time, a rapier fight might entail nothing more than two wide-eyed men running straight at each other, effectively impaling themselves. As Silver wryly suggests, the rhythm of much rapier swordplay of the time might more accurately be described as erratic gasps from two duelists lying on the ground, slowly bleeding to death following a simultaneous kill. Alternatively, there is the more ridiculous example of the fight which never begins. See, for example, Andrew and Viola (III, iv) in *Twelfth Night*.

Rhythm also determines speed. This raises an important qualification. When we speak of fast or faster in describing the typical rapier fight, we are comparing it only to what came before. We believe that an authentic rapier fight would not be breathtakingly fast to a modern audience. There is a simple technical reason for this. Anyone holding a real rapier of the period marvels at its balance, yes, but within seconds the whole affair begins to weigh

quite heavily in the hand. The authors have had rapiers reconstructed based on authentic specimens, and we can say from using
them that though they may weigh only a few pounds, their length
and balance make fight speed dramatically slower. Holding such
a heavy weapon, one can instantly understand why lifting the blade
high overhead is not a smart or even intuitive move.

The rapier blade cannot be twiddled (quick circling of the blade
and point around the opponent's blade) as later short sword and
modern fencing swords allow. On the contrary, rapier blades demand great discipline to align the blade and to keep it aligned at
the enemy, due to its weight and balance. Judging from our own
reconstructed models, rapier play demanded a strong grip and
good forearm strength. The Errol Flynn style of fighting—the
blades whipping and whooshing overhead—which so many associate with this and later styles of fighting is out of the question.

For this reason, we believe that the rapier fights seen in many
modern productions are much too fast. Leonid Tarassuk, a highly
regarded expert in arms and armor history, as well as an experienced fencer, believes that the modern reconstructed rapier fight
is two or three times the true historical speed (personal correspondence, June 16, 1987). Looking at the weapons used to stage most
contemporary theatrical and film fights for this period, we can see
one reason for this: épée fencing blades are often substituted for
the true rapier blade. Also, the hilt is much lighter and smaller.
With the addition of choreography which uses wide, sweeping
blade movements, extreme lunges, and moulinees (circular movements of the weapon over and behind the head from one line of
attack to another), it is easy to see why such increased speeds are
attained.

Offensive Maneuvers

Without recataloging the dozens of offensive movements recommended by the three masters, we can isolate some general principles and techniques common to each. The rapier was only moderately useful in cutting. Cuts were usually aimed at the head or legs
due to padding in the doublet. At most, cutting actions would
only lightly harm the opponent, causing some loss of blood, but

rarely, in the case of a determined adversary, stopping him completely. All three masters (even Silver in his backhanded way) used cutting actions as a supplement to thrusts.

The previous analogy of a tube of space between two rapier stylists opposing each other is helpful here. Since the primary intention of rapier play is to thrust, all effort—even momentary body voids down or to the side—only moves the tube between the fighters to a new angle. The point of the rapier is best left directed at the enemy within this tube, even when parrying.

Within this hypothetical tube, the fighter looks for lines of attack that conveniently remove the danger of the opponent's blade—through evasion of the body or momentary parrying—while at the same time opening up free passage to deliver the kill. The trick is not to lose the constant focus on the opponent's openings.

Parrying and thrusting in simultaneous action comprise an important technique to draw from the fencing manuals. Earlier English sword parries—and short sword parries that were to follow in later centuries—held that the parry was important in and of itself. In rapier play, however, every parry or evasion ideally leads to an immediate attack. This interest in simultaneous parry/attack combinations was derived from the faster pace of the fight as well as the emphasis on point work.

Moreover, the various poses illustrated in this book must be thought of as positions from which an attack may be initiated, rather than basic safe stances. Although Saviolo and Di Grassi go to some length in detailing ways in which the rapier fencer can operate defensively, more attention is paid to effective attacks or quick counters.

Defensive Maneuvers

In the event of attack, the defender's first movement would be a body void. A more skilled rapier fencer would add a simultaneous parry with his blade, thus ensuring that there was absolutely no danger and effectively slowing down the attacker's blade. Finally, at the highest level, a master would void with the body, parry with his blade and return his own attack. Like any highly sophisticated physical skill, such technique would have taken years to perfect.

But once this level was attained, the fencer was truly a master of the rapier.

Of course a typical rapier fight involved all three levels of defensive play. It was not always possible to incorporate simultaneous attacks with parries and voids. As Saviolo specifically points out, even if the rapier fighter's own attacks are not all they should be, he should always be ready to dodge the opponent's attacks. Even the expert would bob, weave, and backpedal to avoid getting hit, relying on good reflexes and cool nerves to earn himself more time.

There are three reasons for assuming that all levels of defensive maneuvers would be operational in a single fight by an individual fighter. First, an expert would not force every opportunity to thrust. He would want a good opening, held long enough that he might reasonably assume completing the kill. He would not want to lapse into the thrusting style of game, simply trading thrusts. Distance and timing are too easily skewed in such fights. A modern equivalent to the waiting game could be the Muhammed Ali or Sugar Ray Leonard style of boxer. Both of these fighters were known for their ability to dance around the boxing ring. They also frequently changed directions around the opponent. Eschewing the more brutal, but often suicidal, method of closing in and just trading punches (as seen in the popular *Rocky* movies), these boxers had long careers. A rapier stylist who also knew how to circle in both directions around an opponent could easily startle and confuse his enemies.

Second, biding time in defensive maneuvering—without feeling the necessity to take advantage of every single offensive opening—might be an excellent way to draw the opponent out far enough to unbalance him. Why emphasize excessive blade contact or risk being hit when, with just a little time and evasion, you might find yourself in perfect position for the killing thrust? We might see a dramatic character like Shakespeare's Mercutio using this technique as a way to put Tybalt off balance and to make fun of him.

Third, as Silver and Saviolo rightly point out, the expert had every reason to fear the uncontrolled movements of a novice. In such a situation, it was better to observe the less-experienced fighter, both to figure out his fighting style and possibly to wear him out a bit (similar to modern Kendo strategy).

Daggers, cloaks, and gloves were popular as supplements to the rapier due to their usefulness in defense. Slapping the opponent's blade away with the empty hand was always a last choice, though preferable when no other parrying tool was available. Using the dagger to firmly parry the incoming blade—by itself or in conjunction with the rapier—increased the specialist's confidence. In addition, as we have noted, the dagger was a superb weapon for fighting in close quarters where the rapier was useless. The cloak effectively made the forearm around which it was wrapped into a shield that could be moved quickly and surely.

An additional critical aspect to defensive rapier play is psychological. Thrusting attacks must have seemed shockingly quick to men used to hacking attacks. A thrust is faster than a cut, as we have discussed. There is also that peculiar and horrific moment that must have filled many a duelist's nightmares: at the completion of a successful thrust, the injured man looks down (assuming the hit wasn't in the face) and sees a thin piece of steel embedded in his body.

Though the hole left by a rapier attack was eerie enough, the chief worry was how severe internal damage had been. Death by a sword could be mercifully quick; the rapier death was a festering, lingering deterioration. The image of such a death, except for the most psychologically prepared, would make even well-practiced moves seem slow and awkward. The characteristic quality of an amateurish fight is one in which both fighters concentrate on avoiding, rather than on attacking. One can imagine two duelists timidly jabbing their blade points at one another, far out of proper distance, and nervously shifting their feet from side to side. Aguecheek and Viola display this behavior in their comic fight in *Twelfth Night*. Indeed, improper distances and tentative extensions are key elements in defining both comic and amateur fighters. Fear of extending the weapon at the wrong moment and opening up to a maddeningly quick return thrust must have been overwhelming.

Strategy

One of the biggest selling points in the distribution or sale of these fencing manuals would have been the buyer's fond hope of finding a secret move that would defeat all opponents. Many fencing masters of the time based their reputations on the whispered talk—real or devised—that there were such techniques. Called the *botte segrete* by the Italians, the secret moves usually referred either to a thrust that could not be parried or to a universal parry that would effectively defend against all thrusts. The cynical reader may wonder if some teachers taught both.

The secret move is a highly romantic and dramatic device, of course, and has often been used in movies and plays to help the hero win at the last minute. Early in Richard Lester's film of *The Three Musketeers*, D'Artagnan—in a rousing sword fight in a barn with his father—is suddenly brought to sword's point by such a surprise tactic. His father tells him that it should be used once and only as a last resort. Naturally, in the momentous climactic fight with Rochefort, D'Artagnan uses the same move.

Like the martial arts lore in other cultures, there had always been teachers in England, as well as in Europe, who developed a mystique based on such surprise moves that would be taught only to their most prized pupils. Since it was up to the master to decide which pupils were prized and which were not, this was a convenient way to ensure strong advertising for the individual schools and to keep the students coming back for more instruction.

Within the three manuals of Di Grassi, Saviolo, and Silver, however, we see no recourse to such questionable tactics. All are quite straightforward in their insistence on the basics of body voiding maneuvers and sound offensive techniques. Silver condemns the practice of secret techniques. All three masters urge the potential student to examine carefully a particular teacher's philosophy regarding real fighting and not just practice bouts.

Published and widely distributed manuals like these would not have included secret techniques. More likely, such books would be purchased or borrowed in anticipation of need, say the night before a duel. We have no record of who directly profited by the sale of these translations, or even if they were sold at all. It is possible that only a small number were printed and distributed to friends and students.

In any case, all three authors convincingly portray their systems as battleworthy and secure. All three manuals agree that any defensive parry should be sustained into an offensive counterstrike. Also, each counsels a simple plan of parrying strategies; none of them has over five basic parries, making them easier to remember and execute. In addition, there is unanimous emphasis on the importance of timing and rhythm as it develops in each fight. The best fighters have a strong sense for proper distance and the exact moment when that distance may be covered in an attack. Ultimately, all three teachers prefer a simple, basic set of movements that can cover a variety of combat situations. Simplicity and consistency in execution are the best strategies.

Theatrical Models

The simplified points we have listed above may serve as reasonably accurate guidelines for reconstructing Elizabethan rapier swordplay. For some choreographers and directors unfamiliar with this material, a new dimension to text references, bits of business, and character relationships should emerge.

A thornier issue may involve the context within which this fight style takes place. If actors are allowed vocal and physical mannerisms more associated with our own time, then the sudden insertion of historically accurate swordplay movement will be confusing. Here, as in most things artistic, it is ultimately the context that should determine the use of these principles.

It may actually take only a few of our suggestions to achieve this verisimilitude of Elizabethan fighting. For example, using circular patterns and thrusting attacks alone should suggest many imaginative new fight patterns. Another possible approach would be using historically accurate weaponry (in regards to weight, length, and shape). This variation will automatically give the choreographer slower movement, more precise attacks, and more emphasis on each thrust. It will certainly provide a challenge to the actors to control such weapons. In any case, whatever elements are chosen, for the serious student of fight history and choreography, it is necessary to take nothing for granted. It is the unconscious modern mannerism or technique that can destroy the integrity of an otherwise carefully conceived reconstruction.

Of course, fight choreographers are subject to the constraints of the productions they work in. We recognize and salute the fight teachers and choreographers who are already attempting to incorporate these elements into their Elizabethan pieces. Despite the limitations of budgets and rehearsal time they are attempting to elevate fight choreography to its true status as handmaiden to theatrical art. For them, we wish this book to be an added source of ideas and inspiration.

Our greatest hope is that producers and directors—as central figures in the theatrical process—will seriously consider these ideas. Incorporating historically accurate fight movement will not only provide insights to textual questions, it will also add new, theatrically exciting elements. At the very least, we wish the whole idea of theatrical violence and its relationship to plays of the period to undergo a serious reappraisal.

Conclusion

Through the last quarter of the sixteenth century, the rapier passed from imported curiosity, to popular fad, to ubiquitous weapon. Though rarely mastered in its time and demanding a unique combination of skill, aggression, and cool-headedness, by 1600, rapier swordplay was highly prized and sought out as the ultimate fighting art by most sophisticated Elizabethans.

In addition, the rapier and rapier play were uniquely related to foreign influences, political intrigue, the decline of the Elizabethan aristocracy, and the flow of cultural artifacts between England and the European nations of the time. Di Grassi, Saviolo, and Silver— with other masters of defense of the time—played out many of these aspects of the Elizabethan world through their efforts to establish standards and training practices for personal self-defense.

Notes

Bibliography

Index

Notes

1. Elizabethan Fencing Masters

1. For a typical example, Genero Pavese, in his *Foil and Sabre Fencing,* claims, "To anyone thoroughly versed in the history of fencing there is not a French guard or position that cannot be traced back to an early period of Italian fencing" (15). Emerson hunts Germanic swordplay back to the Stone Age.

2. In the sixteenth century, with the dissemination of so many books anatomizing the causes and punctilios of the duel, it was possible to "give the lie" for no provocation whatsoever, thus forcing your enemy into challenging you or suffering dishonor. Of course, the challenged party retained the choice of weapons. The situation is satirized by Touchstone in *As You Like It,* whereby a man secure in his fighting ability might force any man to fight him with Saviolo's example, "If any man hath said evil of me, he hath lied: and if he will deny to have said so, he also lieth."

3. Aylward traces legislation banning fencing schools as undesirable places as early as Edward I's reign (1272–1307) (*English Master of Arms* 14).

4. Such as Master Roger Le Skirmisour, jailed in the 1300s for keeping a fencing school of more than dubious character (Aylward, *The English Master of Arms* 9). It may well be that the old military naming of irregular troops—such as mercenary units—as skirmishers may have derived from these troops calling themselves by their profession, i.e., in France, "escrimeur."

5. Salvator Fabris is in many ways the premier example of the widespread influence of the fencing masters and their styles. Leaving politically chaotic Italy, he studied and taught in France. From there he emigrated to Denmark in 1590, under the patronage of King Christian IV. He next accompanied Christian to England when James I ascended the throne; there he witnessed a prizing by the English Masters, probably picking up Saviolo's and Silver's books. He then published his own enormously influential *Sienz e Practica d'Arme* in 1606. He was the new man of the transition

rapier age, which bridges the Elizabethan rapier and dagger and smallsword ages. Whereas Saviolo and Silver are "Shakesperean" fencing masters, Fabris would be the master of Dumas' *The Three Musketeers.*

6. So in *Hamlet* (IV, ii, 241–43) Hamlet says, "I embrace it freely, and will this brother's wager frankly play. Give us the foils." Contrast Laertes' plan to hit Hamlet with "a sword unbated" and poisoned too. A foil might be a blunted weapon, or one that had a button at its point. Castle points out that sometimes a ball of leather or cork about the size of a golf ball might be used to protect the eyes from being put out.

7. Roger Finlay in *Population and Metropolis: The Demography of London, 1580–1650,* estimates London's population in 1580 at 100,000. Some 40 percent of these would be men between the ages of twenty and forty, according to E. A. Wrigley and R. S. Schofield in *The Population History of England, 1541–1871: A Reconstruction.* We have already detailed some of the prominent and influential people of the time involved with Saviolo and his school alone. Some rough analogy of the lasting cultural effect of the Elizabethan fencing master might be made with sixteenth-century Japan. The Samurai class, the western world's sole image of Japan at that time, made up less than 2 percent of the population.

8. Some make it 1567 and Charles IX, some others 1570 and Henri III.

9. Barbasetti gives Marozzo's master as Neppo Bardi, who opened his school at the University of Bologna in 1413 (220).

10. Roger Finlay, in *Population and Metropolis: The Demography of London, 1580–1650* gives the size of the average Elizabethan edition as approximately 1,250 books (354).

11. "1,200 complete armors from Cologne and 2,700 from Antwerp." Norman and Pottinger, *A History of War and Weapons: 449–1600* (150).

12. The right to call the trial by combat was not formally abolished until 1819.

13. "William Joyner's fencing school occupied the blind (or windowless) parlor and the paved hall on the lower floor of the western rectory of Blackfriars precinct and was reached by a passageway off Water Lane. The two rooms, encompassing a space

that was fifty-two feet wide and seventy feet long, were directly below the Parliament Chamber . . . evidence shows Joyner . . . occupying both spaces in 1572. Prior to this time a man named Woodman had an ordinary table in the paved hall and had done some damage to the property. The ordinary could only be reached through the fencing school. Some London ordinaries were notorious gaming houses" (Linda McCollum 14).

    14. Shakespeare scholar A. L. Rowse claims this may have been an anglicization of another Italian fencing master named Brushetti (*The Elizabethan Renaissance* 226).

2. Beginning of the Italian Invasion

    1. Not long before (1578), John Florio, English-born son of an Italian father, had written *Florio His First Fruites*. Used as an Italian-English conversation book, the author calls the English buckler (small shield and short sword fight) a "clownish and dastardly weapon, not fit for a Gentleman" (ff17–18). By Di Grassi's time, the battle for conversion to the rapier had been won.

    2. See especially John Keegan's work, *The Face of Battle*. He discusses the past tendencies of military historians to distance themselves from the realities of combat at the individual level. His chapter on the battle at Agincourt is particularly relevant to our discussions here.

    3. Much of the danger and fear in rapier play came from the ugly nature of such wounds. Even if internal organs were not hit in a thrust, the ragged opening and the almost certain likelihood of infection and internal bleeding made rapier wounds fearsome. Most deaths from dueling occurred long after the fight. See chapter 5 for more of this and its relation to fight psychology.

    4. The earliest simultaneous use of sword and dagger is mentioned by Brantome, referring to a duel which took place at Ferrare in 1512 (Norman 287). Initially, most daggers did not match in design details to the sword, though Norman says there was increased matching between weapons by the end of the century.

    5. The vast majority of daggers made for use with rapiers had a side ring by this time. For an excellent and more detailed analysis

of the development of the dagger as it relates to the rapier, see Leonid Tarassuk's *Parrying Daggers and Poinards.*

3. Vincentio Saviolo: *His Practise in Two Bookes*

1. Castle claims "Carranza and Don Louis Pacheco [Narvaez] were household names in England about the end of the sixteenth century" (73). See also Philip Massinger's *The Unnatural Combat* (II, ii, 11–14): "He can teach our modern Duellists how to cleave a button, and in a new way, never yet found out by old *Caranza.*"

2. His eclecticism is similar to that of Bruce Lee, who studied several martial arts, as well as boxing and fencing, and synthesized the best elements into a new comprehensive combat system he called *Jeet Kune Do.* See his epoch-defining article in *Black Belt* magazine, September, 1971.

3. Viggiani's 1575 book takes the form of a dialogue between "'the most illustrious Signior Luigi Gonzaga . . . and the excellent Messer Lodovico Boccadiferro, philosopher'" (Castle 66). Narvaez's 1612 book in Spain also utilizes a pliant "Disciple" and a wise "Master" in dialogue (Castle 73).

4. A good example of the friendly duel is between Palomon and Arcite in *The Two Noble Kinsmen.*

5. Silver describes the Spanish fight: "they stand as brave as they can with their bodies upright, narrow spaced, with their feet continually moving, as if they were in a dance, *holding forth their arms and rapiers very straight against the face or bodies of their enemies* . . . as long as any man shall lie in that manner with his arm and point of his rapier straight it shall be impossible for his adversary to hurt him" (emphasis added) (Jackson 512).

6. Castle cites Fabris (1606) as the first to define guard in it's modern sense (98). Stone defines it as "A posture, attitude or condition of defense. In fencing, a position of person and sword and certain correlated motions calculated to prevent injury by an opponent" (254).

7. The arms of the hilt are metal guards to protect the fingers passed over the cross-guard or quillons . They are the most distinguishing feature of the rapier, reaching a high degree of sophistication and elaboration in the sixteenth century. Castle defines them

as "a pair of bars, each curved in the form of a loop, added immediately above the cross hilt, on each side of the blade" (Castle 324).

8. The Spanish actually traced out magic circles on the floor, using the diameters, chords, and radii to teach footwork. It was believed that for every movement of the opponent, there was one and only one ultimate corresponding move around the circle that would result in advantage. Study in this school was an attempt to calculate these responses based on the geometry and lore of the master. The mental and physical gymnastics required produced both a supreme coolness in combat and a tendency to be ridiculed for their continual movement, as Silver says, "in manner of dancing" (Jackson 512).

9. Although in discussing Viggiani's book of 1575, Castle acknowledges that Viggiani's punta supramano is very like the modern lunge (66).

10. See Shakespeare's *King Lear* (IV, vi, 240–41), Edgar's "Come. No matter vor your foins." Also *Henry IV, Part Two* (II, i, 16), Hostess about Falstaff, "He will foin like any devil." Also Doll's (II, iv, 215), "wilt thou leave fighting o' days, and foining o' nights." And in *The Merry Wives of Windsor* (II, iii, 21), Host to Caius (rapier in hand), "To see thee fight, to see thee foin." *Much Ado About Nothing* (V, i, 84), Antonio's "Sir boy, I'll whip you from your foining fence."

11. Mercutio's famous taunts in *Romeo and Juliet* (II, iv, 25–26), "the immortal passado, the punto reverso, the hay!" And his "Alla stoccata carries it away!" (III, i, 73). Also Bobadill in Jonson's *Every Man in His Humour* (IV, vii, 71–72): "your *punto*, your *riverso*, your *stoccata*, your *imbroccata*, your *passada*, your *montanto*."

12. A 1971 collegiate fencing glossary defines it as a "counter-offensive action which anticipates and intercepts the final line of the opponent's attack and covers it in that line" (Herdon, 127).

13. John Turner, commissioner of the English Masters, was renowned for hitting his opponents in the eye. Joseph Swetnam notes in his *Schole of the Noble and Worthie Science of Defence* (1617), that Turner killed John Dun by a thrust in the eye. He claims, "Turner by his unlucky hand thrust out two or three eyes, and was

praised by the public for his skill" (Aylward, *The English Master of Arms* 81). John Mannigham in his *Diary* describes it: "Turner and Dun, two famous fencers, played their prizes this day at the bankside, but Turner at last ran Dun so far in the brain at the eye that he fell down presently stone dead; a goodly sport in a Christian state, to see one man kill another" (187). Turner put the Scottish Baron Robert Crichton's eye out in a practice bout. In revenge, Crichton had him assassinated in 1612 (Aylward, *The English Master of Arms* 37).

14. Marozzo (see chapter 1) classifies both mandritti and riversi in four ways: (1) *tondo*—horizontally, (2) *fendente*—vertical downwards, (3) *montante*—vertical upwards, and (4) *sgualembrato*—oblique downwards.

15. Secretly wearing a coat of mail under a shirt, sometimes even painted flesh color (known as supersticerie), became so notorious that in Napoleon's time it was customary to fight naked to the waist.

16. See Selma Guttman's "The Fencing Bout in Hamlet" for a complete and convincing case refuting J. D. Wilson, who maintains that the changing of rapiers can be effected if the scene is played with rapier and dagger.

17. Silver tells us that Bonetti used to make his students wear shoes of lead, to make them lighter and quicker on their feet. It's more than possible that Bonetti, Saviolo, and many of the other masters wore mail shirts for their teaching sessions. The use of a lighter rapier by the masters was also justified in that they wanted their movements to be lighter and quicker, to provide a good example, and they had to teach many students, so a lighter teaching weapon would stave off fatigue a little longer. But these things pass without comment in Saviolo's text, since they are expected in the context of the fencing lesson. The student has enough to concentrate on in learning the basics, and as Saviolo observes, the master should save himself and not hurt his student.

4. The English Reply

1. As early as 1590, John Smythe in his *Certain Discourses Military* showed concern for the increased use of rapiers, even in battle. He accuses military theorists, who should know better, of encouraging

the use of "rapiers of a yard and a quarter long." But in the close quarter of battle "they presently betake themselves to the use of their swords and daggers, which they cannot with any celerity draw if the blades of their swords be so long." And rapier blades "being so narrow and of so small substance" will easily break (43). Additionally, Kelso cites on the part of the upper classes an increasing indifference to military affairs, as compared to earlier times. She speculates that the "long peace . . . had bred a false sense of security" (45).

   2. It appears that even some modern Englishmen have the same resistance to foreign influences. In his *The Sword and the Centuries,* in describing the arrival of the foreign masters to English soil, Alfred Hutton says, "had they been really great masters, what need could there have been for them to travel so far, when travelling was so slow, so difficult, and so costly, when they ought to have been able to gain a handsome living in their own country?" (150).

   3. The notes of the Blackfriars group show us only some of their organizational structure, but none of the skills, techniques, or curricula that were taught.

   4. These ideas are taken from Silver's *Bref Instructions,* never published in his lifetime, and they are included in Jackson's *Three Elizabethan Fencing Manuals.* The manuscript was discovered in the British Museum in 1898 by Captain Cyril G. R. Matthey, also an amateur fencer. Captain Matthey tried to incorporate many of Silver's ideas in a new saber form for the English military.

   5. The authors have observed melees and practice bouts held by the Society for Creative Anachronism. Even in these unschooled modern recreations of medieval fighting, much of this nervous attacking motion may be noted. The impulse of the unskilled fighter is to close quickly, throwing a flurry of attacks in the hope one will connect.

   6. In *Titus Andronicus,* Prince Chiron wields a "daring-rapier," given to him by his mother Tamora. Here it is not the precision of a button-shaving swordsman that is emphasized. Shakespeare's point is that Chiron's very aggressiveness is in part due to having such a weapon.

   7. Aylward says "traditional English dogma [was] that the use of the point dishonours the swordsman" (*English Master of Arms* 2–3).

8. From Bryson's *The Sixteenth-Century Italian Duel:* other fencing specialists felt it was only fair that swords have points since smaller fighters could more easily reach their opponents with a thrust. Bryson specifically cites the advice of Girolamo Muzio in his *Il Duello* (50).

9. From *Bref Instructions*.

10. These are Silver's renderings of what he supposed were the Italian terms. They are not accurate according to Di Grassi, Saviolo, and other Italian referents.

Bibliography

Agrippa, Camillo. *Trattato di scienza d'arme et un dialogo in detta materia.* Venice: Appresso Antonio Pinargenti, 1568.

Angelo, Domenico. *The School of Fencing, With a General Explanation of the Principal Attitudes and Positions Peculiar To the Art.* New York: Land's End Press, 1971.

Ascham, Roger. *The English Works of Roger Ascham.* London: R. and J. Dodsley, 1761.

Aylward, J. D. *The English Master of Arms, from the Twelfth To the Twentieth Century.* London: Routledge and K. Paul, 1956.

———. *The House of Angelo: A Dynasty of Swordsmen.* London: Batchworth Press, 1953.

———. *The Small-Sword in England: Its History, Its Forms, Its Makers, and Its Masters.* London: Hutchinson's Scientific and Technical Publications, 1946.

Baldick, Robert. *The Duel: A History of Duelling.* London: Chapman and Hall, 1965.

Barbasetti, Luigi. *The Art of the Foil, with a Short History of Fencing.* New York: E. P. Dutton, 1932.

Bass, William. *Sword and Buckler: Or, Serving-mans Defence.* London: Privately printed, 1863.

Beaumont, Francis, and John Fletcher. *The Nice Valour. The Works of Francis Beaumont and John Fletcher.* General Editor A. R. Waller. Vol. 10. Cambridge: Cambridge University Press, 1912. 10 Volumes.

Brailsford, Dennis. *Sport and Society: Elizabeth to Anne.* London: Routledge and Kegan Paul, 1969.

Bryson, Frederick Robertson. *The Point of Honor in Sixteenth-Century Italy: An Aspect of the Life of the Gentleman.* Chicago: University of Chicago Libraries, 1935.

———. *The Sixteenth-Century Italian Duel.* Chicago: University of Chicago Press, 1938.

Burton, Richard F. *The Book of the Sword.* London: Chatto and Windus, Piccadilly, 1884.

Capo Ferro, Ridolfo. *Gran simulacro dell'arte e dell'uso della scherma.* Siena: apresso Salvestro Marchetti e Camillo Turi, 1610.

Castle, Egerton. *Schools and Masters of Fence: From the Middle Ages To the Eighteenth Century.* London: Arms and Armour Press, 1969.

Clark, Cumberland. *Shakespeare and Costume.* London: The Mitre Press, 1937.

130   Bibliography

Clephan, Robert Coltman. *The Defensive Armor and the Weapons and Engines of War of Medieval Times, and of the "Renaissance."* London: Walter Scott, Ltd., 1900.

Cowper, Henry S. *The Art of Attack. Being a Study in the Development of Weapons and Appliances of Offense from the Earliest Times to the Age of Gunpowder.* Ulverston: W. Holmes Ltd., 1906.

Craig, Horace S. "Duelling Scenes and Terms in Shakespeare's Plays." *University of California Publications in English* 9 (1940): 1–28.

Demmin, Auguste Frederic. *An illustrated history of arms and armour from the earliest period to the present time.* Translated by C. C. Black. London: Bell and Sons, 1877.

Dessen, Alan C. *Elizabethan Stage Conventions and Modern Interpreters.* Cambridge: Cambridge University Press, 1984.

Diehl, Huston. "The Iconography of Violence in English Renaissance Tragedy." *Renaissance Drama*, n. s. II (1980): 27–44.

Di Grassi, Giacomo. "His True Arte of Defence (1594)." In *Three Elizabethan Fencing Manuals,* edited by James L. Jackson. Delmar, N. Y.: Scholars' Facsimiles and Reprints, 1972.

Dillon, [Viscount]. "Armour and Weapons." In *Shakespeare's England.* General editor Sir Sidney Lee. Volume I. Oxford: Clarendon Press, 1917. 127–40. 2 Volumes.

Docciolini, Marco. *Trattato in materia di scherma.* Florence: Nella stamperia di Michelangelo Sermartelli, 1601.

Emerson, Edwin. *German Swordplay.* Philadelphia: Graf and Breuninger, 1936.

Fabris, Salvator. *Sienz e Practica d'Arme.* Copenhagen: Henrico Waltkirch, 1606.

Ffoulkes, Charles John. *Armour and Weapons.* Oxford: The Clarendon Press, 1909.

———. *The Armourer and His Craft.* London: Methuen and Co., 1912.

Finlay, Roger. *Population and Metropolis: The Demography of London, 1580–1650.* Cambridge: Cambridge University Press, 1981.

Gardner, John. *Armor in England from the earliest times to the reign of James the First.* London: Seeley and Co., Ltd., 1897.

Gardner, Robert E. *Five Centuries of Gunsmiths, Swordsmiths and Armourers, 1400–1900.* Columbus, Ohio: W. F. Heer, 1948.

Gies, Frances. *The Knight in History.* New York: Harper and Row, 1984.

Giganti, Nicoletto V. *Scola overo teatro nel qual sono rappresentate diverse maniere e modi di parare et di ferire di spada sola . . . professione dell'Armi.* Venice, 1606.

Gilbert, Humphrey. *Queen Elizabethes Achademy.* Edited by F. J. Furnivall. London: K. Paul Trench, Trubner, and Co., 1898.

Graves, Thornton S. "The Stage Sword and Dagger." *South Atlantic Quarterly* 20 (1921): 201–12.

Gurr, Andrew. *Playgoing in Shakespeare's London.* Cambridge: Cambridge University Press, 1987.

Guttman, Selma. "The Fencing Bout in Hamlet." *The Shakespeare Associa-tion Bulletin* 14 (1939): 82–100.

Hale, J. R. "The Military Education of the Officer Class." In *Renaissance War Studies*. London: The Hambledon Press, 1983.

———. *War and Society in Renaissance Europe, 1450–1620*. New York: St. Martin's Press, 1985.

Harbage, Alfred. *Shakespeare's Audience*. New York: Columbia University Press, 1969.

Herdon, Myrtis. *Selected Fencing Articles*. Washington, D.C., 1971.

Hole, Christina. *English Sports and Pastimes*. London: B. T. Batsford, Ltd., 1949.

Holmes, Martin R. *Arms and Armour in Tudor and Stuart London*. Lon-don: H. M. S. O., 1970.

———. *Elizabethan London*. London: Cassell and Company, Ltd., 1969.

Hussey, Jeanette M. *The Code Duello*. Washington, D. C.: Smithsonian Press, 1980.

Hutton, Alfred. *Old Sword-Play: the system of fence in vogue during the xvith, xviith, and xviiith Centuries, with Lessons arranged from the works of various ancient masters*. London: H. Grevel and Co., 1892.

———. *The Sword and the Centuries: or, Old Sword Days and Old Sword Ways*. Vermont: Charles E. Tuttle Co., 1980.

Jackson, James L., ed. *Three Elizabethan Fencing Manuals*. Delmar, N. Y.: Scholars' Facsimiles and Reprints, 1972.

Jonson, Ben. *The New Inn*. Edited by Michael Hattaway. Dover, N.H.: Manchester University Press, 1984.

Keegan, John. *The Face of Battle*. New York: Penguin Books, 1986.

Kelso, Ruth. *The Doctrine of the English Gentleman in the Sixteenth Century*. Gloucester, Mass.: Peter Smith, 1964.

Laking, Guy F. *A Record of European Armor and Arms Through Seven Centuries*. London: G. Bell and Sons, Ltd., 1922.

Laneham, Robert. *Robert Laneham's Letter: Describing a Part of the Enter-tainment Unto Queen Elizabeth at the Castle of Kesilworth in 1575*. New Shakespeare Society, series 6, no. 14. Edited by F. J. Furnivall. London, 1907.

Lee, Sidney, ed. *Shakespeare's England*. Oxford: Clarendon Press, 1917.

Machyn, Henry. *The Diary of Henry Machyn, citizen and merchant-taylor of London, from A.D. 1550 to A.D. 1563*. Edited by John Gough Nichols. London: J. B. Nichols and Son, 1848.

MacIntyre, Jean. "Shakespeare and the Battlefield: Tradition and Innova-tion in Battle Scenes." *Theatre Survey* 23 (1982): 31–44.

Manley, Albert. *Complete Fencing*. New York: Doubleday and Company, Inc., 1979.

Manningham, John. *The Diary of John Manningham of the Middle Temple, 1602–1603*. Edited by Robert Parker Sorlein. Hanover, N.H.: Uni-versity Press of New England, 1976.

Marozzo, Achille. *Opera Nova*. Modene: Antonio Bergola, 1536.

Martines, Lauro, ed. "Introduction: The Historical Approach to Violence." In *Violence and Civil Disorder in Italian Cities, 1200–1500.* Berkeley: University of California Press, 1972.

Massinger, Philip. *The Unnatural Combat.* Edited by Robert Stockdale Telfer. Princeton, N.J.: The Princeton University Press, 1932.

McCollum, John I., Jr., ed. *The Age of Elizabeth.* Boston: Houghton Mifflin Company, 1960.

McCollum, Linda. "Rocco Bonetti." *The Fight Master: Journal of the Society of American Fight Directors* 9 (May 1986): 13–17.

Morsberger, Robert E. "Swordplay and the Elizabethan and Jacobean Stage." *Salzburg Studies in Elizabethan Literature.* Edited by James Hogg. 37 (1974): 1–129.

Nadi, Aldo. *On Fencing.* New York: G. P. Putnam's Sons, 1943.

Nichols, John Gough, ed. *Literary Remains of King Edward the Sixth.* Vol. II. London: J. B. Nichols and Sons, 1857.

Norman, A. V. B. *The Rapier and Small-Sword, 1460–1820.* New York: Arno Press, 1980.

Norman, A. V. B., and Pottinger, Don. *A History of War and Weapons, 449–1660.* New York: Thomas Y. Crowell Co., 1966.

Oakeshott, R. Ewart. *European Weapons and Armour: From the Renaissance to the Industrial Revolution.* Guildford: Lutterworth Press, 1980.

Oman, C. W. C. *The Art of War in the Middle Ages: A.D. 378–1515.* Ithaca, N.Y.: Cornell University Press, 1986.

Palffy-Alpar, Julius. *Sword and Masque.* Philadelphia: F. A. Davis Co., 1967.

Palliser, D. M. *The Age of Elizabeth: England Under the Later Tudors: 1547–1603.* London: Longman, 1983.

Pavese, Genero. *Foil and Sabre Fencing.* Baltimore: King Bros., 1905.

Pollock, Frederick. *The Forms and History of the Sword.* London: Oxford Lectures, 1890.

Powell, George H. *Duelling Stories of the Sixteenth Century: From the French of Brantome.* London: A. H. Bullen, 1904.

Rondelle, Louis. *Foil and Sabre, A Grammar of Fencing.* Boston, 1892.

Rowse, A. L. *The Elizabethan Renaissance.* New York: Scribner, 1971.

Russell, Douglas A. *Period Style for the Theatre.* Boston: Allyn and Bacon, Inc., 1980.

Sainct Didier, Henry de. *Traicte contenant les secrets . . . sur l'espee.* Paris: Society du livre d'art ancien et moderne, 1907.

Saviolo, Vincentio. "His Practise." In *Three Elizabethan Fencing Manuals,* edited by James L. Jackson. Delmar, N.Y.: Scholars' Facsimiles and Reprints, 1972, 187–488.

Segar, William. *The Book of Honor and Armes (1590) and Honor Military and Civil (1602).* Edited by Diane Bornstein. Delmar, N.Y.: Scholars' Facsimiles and Reprints, 1975.

Selden, John. *The Duello, or, Single Combat: From Antiquity derived into this Kingdom of England: With several Kinds and Ceremonies and Forms thereof from good Authority described.* London: William Bzay, 1610. Reprint 1711.

Shakespeare, William. *The Complete Pelican Shakespeare.* General editor Alfred Harbage. Baltimore: Penguin Books, 1971.

Sieveking, A. Forbes. "Fencing and Duelling." In *Shakespeare's England.* General editor Sidney Lee. Volume 2. Oxford: Clarendon Press, 1917, 389–407. 2 Vols.

Silver, George. "Paradoxes of Defence" and "Bref Instructions Upon My Paradoxes of Defence." In *Three Elizabethan Fencing Manuals,* edited by James L. Jackson. Delmar, N.Y.: Scholars' Facsimiles and Reprints, 1972, 489–634.

Smith, Irwin. *Shakespeare's Blackfriars Playhouse: Its History and Design.* New York University Press, 1964.

Smith, Lacey Baldwin. *The Horizon Book of the Elizabethan World.* Edited by Norman Kotker. New York: American Heritage Publishing Co., Inc., 1967.

Smythe, John. *Certain Discourses Military.* Edited by J. R. Hale. Ithaca, N.Y.: 1964.

Soens, A. L. "Cudgels and Rapiers: The Staging of the Edgar-Oswald Fight in Lear." *Shakespeare Studies* 5 (1969): 149–58.

Steinmetz, Andrew. *The Romance of Duelling in All Times and Countries.* Volume 1. London, 1868.

Stone, Lilly C. *English Sports and Recreation.* Washington, D.C.: The Folger Shakespeare Library, 1979.

Tarassuk, Leonid. *Parrying Daggers and Poniards.* Blue Diamond, Nev.: The Society of American Fight Directors, 1987.

Tarassuk, Leonid, and Claude Blair. *The Complete Encyclopedia of Arms & Weapons.* New York: Simon and Schuster, 1982.

Thimm, Carl A. *Bibliography of Fencing and Duelling.* New York: Benjamin Blom, Inc., 1968.

Thornbury, George Walter, ed. *Shakespeare's England; or, Sketches of our Social History in the Reign of Elizabeth.* 2 volumes. London: Longman, Brown, Green and Longmans, 1856.

Tillyard, E. M. W. *The Elizabethan World Picture.* New York: Macmillan Co., 1944.

Vale, Marcia. *The Gentleman's Recreations.* Cambridge: D. S. Brewer Ltd., 1977.

Valentine, Eric. *Rapiers: An Illustrated Reference Guide To the Rapiers of the 16th and 17th Centuries With Their Companions.* Harrisburg, Pa: Stackpole Books, 1968.

Wagner, Eduard. *Cut and Thrust Weapons.* London: Spring Books, 1967.

Wilson, J. Dover. "Introduction." In *George Silver's Paradoxes of Defence, 1599.* London: Oxford University Press, 1933.

Wise, Arthur. *The Art and History of Personal Combat*. Greenwich, Conn: Arma Press, 1972.

———. *Weapons in the Theatre*. New York: Barnes and Noble, 1969.

Wise, Terence. *Medieval Warfare*. New York: Hastings House, 1976.

Wrigley, E. A., and R. S. Schofield. *The Population History of England, 1541–1871: A Reconstruction*. Cambridge: Harvard University Press, 1981.

Youings, Joyce. "Rebellion, Commotions, Lawbreaking and Litigation." In *Sixteenth Century England*. London: Allen Lane, 1984.

Index

Craig Turner is Associate Professor, Director of Graduate Studies, and head of movement training for the Professional Actor Training Program at the University of North Carolina–Chapel Hill. In addition to his classes in the conservatory graduate program, he also serves as company movement coach for Playmakers Repertory Company, a major regional theatre affiliated with the professional program. He has choreographed fights for stage and television, in addition to acting in and directing numerous professional and university productions. He is an affiliate of the Society of American Fight Directors. He has also published research and lectured on movement analysis, mask theory/performance, and the application of martial arts principles to western actor training.

Tony Soper is an actor and fight director, certified with recommendation by the Society of American Fight Directors. As both actor and fight director he has worked in regional theatres across the country, from the New York Shakespeare Festival to the Seattle Repertory Theatre. He has trained with the National Kabuki Theatre of Japan and with noted fight masters Patrick Crean of Canada and Malcolm Ransom of Britain, and with America's S.A.F.D. masters. His special area of interest has been the fusion of Asian stage combat techniques with Western (particularly Shakespearean) weapons styles.